INSIGHT GUIDES

GERMAN

PHRASEBOOK & DICTIONARY

Contacting the Editors

Every effort has been made to provide accurate information in this publication, but changes are inevitable. The publisher cannot be responsible for any resulting loss, inconvenience or injury. We would appreciate it if readers would call our attention to any errors or outdated information. We also welcome your suggestions; if you come across a relevant expression not in our phrase book, please contact us at: hello@insightguides.com

All Rights Reserved
© 2015 APA Publications (UK) Ltd.

First Edition: 2015
Printed in China

Cover & Interior Design: Pawel Pasternak
Production: AM Services
Production Manager: Vicky Glover
Picture Researcher: Slawek Krajewski
Cover Photo: all iStockphoto

Interior Photos: all iStockphoto

CONTENTS

FOOD & DRINK

GOING OUT

DICTIONARY

PRONUNCIATION

This section is designed to make you familiar with the sounds of German, using our simplified phonetic transcription. You'll find the pronunciation of the German letters explained below, together with their 'imitated' equivalents. This system is used throughout the phrase book; simply read the pronunciation as if it were English, noting any special rules below.

The German alphabet is the same as English, with the addition of the letter **ß**. Some vowels appear with an **Umlaut**: **ä**, **ü** and **ö**. Of note, German recently underwent a spelling reform. The letter **ß** is now shown as **ss** after a short vowel, but is unchanged after a long vowel or diphthong. In print and dated material, you may still see the **ß**; e.g., formerly **Kuß**, now **Kuss**.

Stress has been indicated in the phonetic transcription: the underlined letters should be pronounced with more stress, e.g., *Adresse, ah-drehs-uh.*

CONSONANTS

Letter	Approximate Pronunciation	Symbol	Example	Pronunciation
b	1. at the end of a word or between a vowel and a consonant, like p in up	**p**	**ab**	*ahp*
	2. elsewhere, as in English	**b**	**bis**	*bihs*
c	1. before e, i, ä and ö, like ts in hits	**ts**	**Celsius**	*tsehl•see•oos*
	2. elsewhere, like c in cats	**k**	**Café**	*kah•feh*
ch	1. like k in kit	**k**	**Wachs**	*vahks*
	2. after vowels, like ch in Scottish loch	**kh**	**doch**	*dohkh*

Letter	Approximate Pronunciation	Symbol	Example	Pronunciation
d	1. at the end of the word or before a consonant, like t in eat	t	**Rad**	*raht*
	2. elsewhere, like d in do	d	**danke**	*dahn•kuh*
g	1. at the end of a word, sounds like k	k	**fertig**	*<u>fehr</u>•teek*
	2. like g in go	g	**gehen**	*<u>geh</u>•uhn*
j	like y in yes	y	**ja**	*yah*
qu	like k + v in onion	kv	**Quark**	*kvahrk*
r	pronounced in the back of the mouth	r	**warum**	*vah•<u>room</u>*
s	1. before or vowels, like z in zoo	z	**sie**	*zee*
	2. before p and t, like sh in shut	sh	**Sport**	*shpohrt*
	3. elsewhere, like s in sit	s	**es ist**	*ehs ihst*
ß	like s in sit	s	**groß**	*grohs*
sch	like sh in shut	sh	**schnell**	*shnehl*
tsch	like ch in chip	ch	**deutsch**	*doych*
tz	lke ts in hits	ch	**Platz**	*plahts*
v	1. like f in for	f	**vier**	*feer*
	2. in foreign words, like v i voice	v	**Vase**	*<u>vah</u>•seh*
w	like v in voice	v	**wie**	*vee*
z	like ts in hits	ts	**zeigen**	*<u>tsie</u>•gehn*

Letters f, h, k, l, m, n, p, t and x are pronounced as in English.

VOWELS

Letter	Approximate Pronunciation	Symbol	Example	Pronunciation
a	like a in father	**ah**	**Tag**	*tahk*
ä	1. like e in let	**eh**	**Lärm**	*lehrm*
	2. like a in late	**ay**	**spät**	*shpayt*
e	1. like e in let	**eh**	**schnell**	*shnehl*
	2. at the end of a word, if the syllable is not stressed, like u in us	**uh**	**bitte**	<u>*biht*</u> • *tuh*
i	1. like i in hit, before a doubled consonant	**ih**	**billig**	*bih* • *leek*
	2. otherwise, like ee in meet	**ee**	**ihm**	*eem*
o	like o in home	**oh**	**voll**	*fohl*
ö	like o in fern	**er**	**schön**	*shern*
u	like oo in boot	**oo**	**Nuss**	*noos*
ü	like ew in new	**er**	**über**	<u>*ew*</u> • *behr*
y	like ew in new	**ew**	**typisch**	<u>*tew*</u> • *peesh*

COMBINED VOWELS

Letter	Approximate Pronunciation	Symbol	Example	Pronunciation
ai, ay **ei, ey**	like ie in tie	**ie**	**nein**	*nien*
ao, au	like ow in now	**ow**	**auf**	*owf*
äu, eu **oy**	like oy in boy oy	**oy**	**neu**	*noy*

HOW TO USE THE APP

Quickly access your recently viewed entries

Look up words and phrases on-the-go

Conveniently navigate the phrasebook categories

No SIM

18:02

INSIGHT GUIDES

Insight Guides German Phrasebook

tting Started >

ploring >

ivities >

Health and Safety >

Food and Drink >

Menu reader

Going Out

Change font size and background color

Phrasebook Tools Catalogue Favourites Info

Save the most useful everyday words and phrases to your Favorites

Use the Flash Cards Quiz to learn and memorize new words easily

Take all digital advantages of the app: listen to words and phrases pronounced by native speakers

To learn how to activate the app, see the inside back cover of this phrasebook.

THE BASICS

GRAMMAR

REGULAR VERBS

Regular verbs in German are conjugated as in the table below.
Note that the past is expressed with **haben** (to have) or **sein** (to
be) plus the past participle. The future is formed with **werden**
(will) plus the infinitive.

BEZAHLEN	FDH	PRESENT	PAST	FUTURE
I	ich	bezahle	habe bezahlt	*werde bezahlen*
you (inf.)	du	bezahlst	hast bezahlt	*wirst bezahlen*
he/she/it	er/sie/es	bezahlt	hat bezahlt	*wird bezahlen*
we	wir	bezahlen	haben bezahlt	*werden bezahlen*
you (pl.) (inf.) *werdet*	ihr	bezahlt	habt bezahlt	*bezahlen*
they/you	sie/Sie	bezahlen	haben bezahlt	*werden bezahlen*

Example: **Ich bezahle bar.** I'll pay in cash.
Er *m* **/sie** *f* **bezahlt mit Kreditkarte.** He/She will pay with credit
card.

MACHEN	FDH	PRESENT	PAST	FUTURE
I	ich	mache	**habe gemacht**	*werde machen*
you (inf.)	du	machst	**hast gemacht**	**wirst machen**
he/she/it	er/sie/es	macht	**hat gemacht**	*wird machen*
we	wir	machen	**haben gemacht**	*werden machen*
you (pl.) (inf.)	ihr	macht	**habt gemacht**	*werdet machen*
they/you	sie/Sie	machen	**haben gemacht**	*werden machen*

Examples: **Ich mache hier Urlaub.** I'm here on vacation.
Was machen Sie beruflich? What do you do (for work)?

IRREGULAR VERBS

There are a number of irregular verbs in German. Two common irregular verbs in German are **haben** (to have) and **sein** (to be). Conjugations follow:

HABEN	FDH	PRESENT	PAST	FUTURE
I	ich	habe	**habe gehabt**	*werde haben*
you (inf.)	du	hast	**hast gehabt**	*wirst haben*
he/she/it	er/sie/es	hat	**hat gehabt**	*wird haben*
we	wir	haben	**haben gehabt**	*werden haben*
you (pl.) (inf.)	ihr	habt	**habt gehabt**	*werdet haben*
they/you	sie/Sie	haben	**haben gehabt**	*werden haben*

Example: **Ich habe einen Koffer.** I have one suitcase.
Ihr habt viel zu tun. You guys have a lot to do.

SEIN	FDH	PRESENT	PAST	FUTURE
I	ich	bin	bin gewesen	*werde sein*
you (inf.)	du	bist	bist gewesen	*wirst sein*
he/she/it	er/sie/es	ist	ist gewesen	*wird sein*
we	wir	sind	sind gewesen	*werden sein*
you (pl.) (inf.)	ihr	seid	seid gewesen	*werdet sein*
they/you	sie/Sie	sind	sind gewesen	*werden sein*

Example: **Ich bin geschäftlich hier.** I am here on business.
Wir sind glücklich. We are happy.

WORD ORDER

German is similar to English in terms of word order for simple
sentences; it follows the subject-verb-object pattern.
Example: **Wir lassen unser Gepäck hier.** We leave our luggage
here.
When the sentence doesn't begin with a subject, the word order
changes: the verb and the subject are inverted.
Examples:

Er	ist	in Berlin.		He is in Berlin.
Heute	ist	er	in Berlin.	Today he is in Berlin.
	Wir	sind	in Berlin gewesen.	We were in Berlin.

To ask a question, begin with the verb and follow with the
subject, as in English. Example: **Seid ihr in Köln gewesen?**
Have you been to Cologne? (Literally: Have you to Cologne
been?)

NEGATION

The negative is formed in German by putting **nicht** after the verb.

Example: **Ich bin Thomas**. I am Thomas.
Ich bin nicht Thomas. I am not Thomas.

If a noun is used, the negation is made by adding **kein** (masculine and neuter), or **keine** (feminine). For plural nouns, always add **keine**.

Example: **Wir haben keine Einzelzimmer.**
We don't have any single rooms.

IMPERATIVES

Whereas in English the imperative always looks like the infinitive ('Go!'), in German it is derived from the **du-/Sie-** form of the present tense. In the **du-** form, the **-st** is dropped.

All other forms are identical to the present tense. Note that the verb always comes first in commands.

		Go!
du	you (inf.)	**Geh!**
ihr	you (pl.) (inf.)	**Geht!**
Sie	you	**Gehen Sie!**
wir	we	**Gehen wir!** (Let's go!)

NOUNS & ARTICLES

In German, all nouns are capitalized. German nouns are also gender-specific; they can be masculine, feminine or neuter. There is no easy way to determine whether a noun is masculine, feminine or neuter.

There are three definite articles (the) in German: **der**, **die** and **das**. Masculine words use **der**, feminine words use **die** and neuter words use **das**.

The only way to tell whether a word is masculine, feminine or neuter is to look at the article. For this reason, it is best to memorize the article when learning the word. For plural nouns using a definite article, all genders use **die**.

Definite examples: **der Mann** (the man), **die Männer** (the men); **die Frau** (the woman), **die Frauen** (the women); **das Kind** (neuter) (the child), **die Kinder** (neuter) (the children)
There are four cases in German. The definite articles are as follows:

	Masculine	Feminine	Neuter	Plural (all genders)
nominative	der	die	das	die
accusative	den	die	das	die
dative	dem	der	dem	den
genitive	des	der	des	der

German uses two indefinite articles (a/an): **ein** and **eine**. Masculine and neuter nouns use **ein**, and feminine nouns use **eine**.

For plural nouns, the indefinite article is dropped, as in English. Indefinite examples include: **ein Zug** (a train), **Züge** (trains); **eine Karte** (a map), **Karten** (maps)

ADJECTIVES

Adjectives must agree with the nouns they modify. Adjective
endings change based on the article used and the case.
For masculine nouns, **–er** is added to the adjective after an
indefinite article and **–e** is added after a definite article.
Example: **ein kleiner Herr** a short gentleman
der kleine Herr the short gentleman
For feminine nouns, **–e** is added to the adjective after both an
indefinite and a definite article.
Example: **eine kluge Frau** an intelligent woman
die kluge Frau the intelligent woman
For neuter nouns, **–es** is added to the adjective after an
indefinite article, while **–e** is added to the adjective after a
definite article.
Example: **ein großes Land** a big country
das große Land the big country

COMPARATIVES & SUPERLATIVES

In German, the comparative of an adjective is usually formed by
adding **–er** to the end of the adjective.
Examples: **klein** (small), **kleiner** (smaller); **billig** (cheap), **billiger**
(cheaper); **groß** (big), **größer** (bigger)
The superlative is formed by adding **–sten** or **–esten** to the end
of the adjective. If the adjective has a vowel of **a**, **o** or **u**, it may
change to **ä**, **ö** or **ü** in the comparative and superlative forms.
Examples: **klein** (small), **kleinsten** (smallest); **billig** (cheap),
billigsten (cheapest); **groß** (big); **größten** (biggest)

POSSESSIVE ADJECTIVES

Possessive adjectives must agree in gender and number with the noun they are associated with.

	Singular Masculine/ Neuter	Feminine	Plural
my	mein	meine	meine
your (inf.)	dein	deine	deine
his/its	sein	seine	seine
her/their	ihr	ihre	ihre
your (pl.) (inf.)	Ihr	Ihre	Ihre
our	unser	unsere	unsere

Example: **Wir lassen unser Gepäck im Hotel.** We leave our luggage in the hotel.

POSSESSIVE PRONOUNS

Possessive pronouns agree in gender and number with the noun they replace.

	Masculine	Feminine	Neuter
mine	meiner	meine	meines
yours (inf.)	deiner	deine	deines
his/its	seiner	seine	seines
hers/theirs	ihrer	ihre	ihres
ours	unserer	unsere	unseres
yours (pl.) (inf.)	eurer	eure	eures

Example: **Wem gehört der Schlüssel?** Whose key is this? **Das ist meiner.** It's mine.

ADVERBS & ADVERBIAL EXPRESSIONS

In German, adverbs are usually identical to adjectives but, unlike adjectives, their endings don't change.
Examples:
Adjective: **das gute Essen** the good food
Adverb: **Sie sprechen gut Deutsch.** You speak German well.

GETTING STARTED

THE BASICS

NUMBERS

NEED TO KNOW

0	**null**	*nool*
1	**eins**	*iens*
2	**zwei**	*tsvie*
3	**drei**	*drie*
4	**vier**	*feer*
5	**fünf**	*fewnf*
6	**sechs**	*zehks*
7	**sieben**	*zeeb•uhn*
8	**acht**	*ahkht*
9	**neun**	*noyn*
10	**zehn**	*tsehn*
11	**elf**	*ehlf*
12	**zwölf**	*tsverlf*

13	**dreizehn**
	driet • sehn
14	**vierzehn**
	feert • sehn
15	**fünfzehn**
	fewnf • tsehn
16	**sechszehn**
	zehk • tsehn
17	**siebzehn**
	zeep • tsehn
18	**achtzehn**
	ahkht • tsehn
19	**neunzehn**
	noyn • tsehn
20	**zwanzig**
	tsvahnt • seek
21	**einundzwanzig**
	ien • oond • tsvahn • tseek
22	**zweiundzwanzig**
	tsvie • oond • tsvahn • tseek
30	**dreißig**
	drie • seekh
31	**einunddreißig**
	ien • oont • drie • seekh
40	**vierzig**
	feert • seek
50	**fünfzig**
	fewnf • tseeg
60	**sechzig**
	zehkht • seeg
70	**siebzig**
	zeeb • tseeg

80	**achtzig**	
	ahkht • tseeg	
90	**neunzig**	
	noynt • seek	
100	**einhundert**	
	ien • hoon • dehrt	
101	**einhunderteins**	
	ien • hoon • dehr • tiens	
200	**zweihundert**	
	tsvie • hoon • dehrt	
500	**fünfhundert**	
	fewnf • hoon • dehrt	
1,000	**eintausend**	
	ien • tow • zuhnt	
10,000	**zehntausend**	
	tsehn • tow • zuhnt	
1,000,000	**eine Million**	
	ien • uh mihl • yohn	

ORDINAL NUMBERS

first	**erste**	
	ehrs • tuh	
second	**zweite**	
	tsviet • uh	
third	**dritte**	
	driht • tuh	
fourth	**vierte**	
	feer • tuh	
fifth	**fünfte**	
	fewnf • tuh	

once	**einmal**
	ien • mahl
twice	**zweimal**
	tsvie • mahl
three times	**dreimal**
	drie • mahl

TIME

NEED TO KNOW

What time is it?	**Wie spät ist es?**
	vee shpayt ihst ehs
It's midday.	**Es ist zwölf.**
	ehs ihst tsverlf
At midnight.	**Um Mitternacht.**
	oom miht • tehr • nahkht
From one o'clock to two o'clock.	**Von eins bis zwei.**
	fohn iens bihs tsvie
Five past three.	**Fünf nach drei.**
	fewnf nahkh drie
A quarter to four.	**Viertel vor vier.**
	feert • uhl fohr feer
5:30 a.m./5:30 p.m.	**Fünf Uhr dreißig/Siebzehn Uhr dreißig**
	fewnf oohr drie • seeg/zeeb • tsuhn oohr drie • seeg

(i)

Germans use the 24-hour clock in formal contexts (radio, TV, transportation schedules and digital clocks) or when confusion might otherwise arise. The morning hours from 1:00 a.m. to noon are the same as in English. After that, just add 12: so 1:00 p.m. would be 13:00, 5:00 p.m. would be 17:00 and so on. This system eliminates the necessity of 'a.m.' and 'p.m.' markers. When the 12-hour clock is used, **morgens** (in the morning) and **abends** (in the evening) are added after the number for clarity.

DAYS

NEED TO KNOW

Monday	**Montag**
	mohn • tahk
Tuesday	**Dienstag**
	deens • tahk
Wednesday	**Mittwoch**
	miht • vohhk
Thursday	**Donnerstag**
	dohn • ehrs • tahk
Friday	**Freitag**
	frie • tahk
Saturday	**Samstag**
	zahms • tahk
Sunday	**Sonntag**
	zohn • tahk

DATES

yesterday	**gestern**
	gehs • tehrn
today	**heute**
	hoy • tuh
tomorrow	**morgen**
	mohr • guhn
day	**Tag**
	tahk
week	**Woche**
	vohkh • uh
month	**Monat**
	moh • naht
year	**Jahr**
	yahr

ⓘ

German calendars and weeks, like the U.K., are arranged Monday through Sunday (in contrast to the U.S., where calendars run Sunday through Saturday).

MONTHS

January	**Januar**
	yahn • wahr
February	**Februar**
	fehb • rooahr
March	**März**
	mehrts
April	**April**
	ah • prihl

May	**Mai** *mie*
June	**Juni** *yoo • nee*
July	**Juli** *yoo • lee*
August	**August** *ow • goost*
September	**September** *zehp • tehm • behr*
October	**Oktober** *ohk • toh • behr*
November	**November** *noh • vehm • behr*
December	**Dezember** *deh • tsehm • behr*

SEASONS

in...	**im ...** *ihm ...*
spring	**Frühling** *frewh • leeng*
summer	**Sommer** *zohm • ehr*
fall [autumn]	**Herbst** *hehrbst*
winter	**Winter** *vihnt • ehr*

HOLIDAYS

January 1: New Year's Day, **Neujahrstag**
January 6: Epiphany, **Heilige Drei Könige**
May 1: Labor Day, **Tag der Arbeit**
August 15: Assumption Day, **Mariä Himmelfahrt**
October 3: German Unity Day, **Tag der Deutschen Einheit**
November 1: All Saint's Day, **Allerheiligen**
December 25: Christmas, **Erster Weihnachtstag**
December 26: St. Stephen's Day [Boxing Day], **Zweiter Weihnachtstag**
The Easter (movable) holidays are:
Ascension Day, **Christ Himmelfahrt**
Easter Sunday, **Ostersonntag**
Easter Monday, **Ostermontag**
Feast of Corpus Christi, **Fronleichnam**
Good Friday, **Karfreitag**
Pentecost, **Pfinstsonntag**
Pentecost Monday, **Pfinstmontag**

One of Germany's most famous festivals is **Oktoberfest**, held each September in Munich. This food and beer festival extends for more than two weeks and is attended by about six million visitors from around the world. Another popular festival is **Karneval**, celebrated with parades and parties the week before Lent in areas that have substantial Catholic populations. Christmas festivities and markets are also very popular in Germany. Locals and tourists alike visit these markets to purchase local handmade crafts such as toys, wooden carvings, marionettes, candles, lambskin shoes and much more. There are plenty of food vendors available with numerous tasty treats to try.

ARRIVAL & DEPARTURE

NEED TO KNOW

I'm on vacation [holiday].	**Ich mache Urlaub.** *eekh mahkh • uh oor • lowb*
I'm on business.	**Ich bin auf Geschäftsreise.** *eekh bihn owf guh • shehfts • rie • zuh*
I'm going to…	**Ich reise nach …** *eekh rie • zuh nahkh …*
I'm staying at the…Hotel.	**Ich übernachte im Hotel …** *eekh ew • buhr • nahkh • tuh ihm hoh • tehl …*

YOU MAY HEAR…

Ihren Reisepass, bitte.
eer • uhn rie • zuh • pahs biht • tuh
Your passport, please.

Was ist der Grund Ihrer Reise?
vahs ihst dehr groont ihr • uhr rie • zuh
What's the purpose of your visit?

Wo übernachten Sie?
voh ew • behr • nahkh • tuhn zee
Where are you staying?

Wie lange bleiben Sie? *vee lahng • uh blie • buhn zee*
How long are you staying?

Mit wem reisen Sie?
miht vehm rie • zuhn zee
Who are you traveling with?

BORDER CONTROL

I'm just passing through.	**Ich bin auf der Durchreise.**
	eekh been owf dehr <u>doorkh</u> • rie • zuh
I'd like to declare…	**Ich möchte … verzollen.**
	eekh <u>merkh</u> • tuh … fehr • <u>tsoh</u> • luhn
I have nothing to declare.	**Ich habe nichts zu verzollen.**
	eekh <u>hah</u> • buh neekhts tsoo fehr • <u>tsoh</u> • luhn

YOU MAY HEAR…

Haben Sie etwas zu verzollen?	Do you have anything to declare?
hah • buhn zee <u>eht</u> • vahs tsoo fehr • <u>tsoh</u> • luhn	
Darauf müssen Sie Zoll zahlen.	You must pay duty on this.
dahr • <u>owf mew</u> • suhn zee tsol <u>tsah</u> • luhn	
Öffnen Sie diese Tasche.	Open this bag.
erf • nuhn zee <u>dee</u> • zuh <u>tah</u> • shuh	

YOU MAY SEE…

ZOLL	customs
ZOLLFREIE WAREN	duty-free goods
ZOLLPFLICHTIGE WAREN	goods to declare
NICHTS ZU VERZOLLEN	nothing to declare
PASSKONTROLLE	passport control
POLIZEI	police

MONEY

NEED TO KNOW

Where's...?	**Wo ist ...?**
	voh ihst ...
the ATM	**der Bankautomat**
	dehr <u>bahnk</u> • ow • toh • maht
the bank	**die Bank**
	dee bahnk
the currency	**die Wechselstube**
exchange office	*dee <u>vehkh</u> • zuhl • shtoo • buh*
When does the	**Wann öffnet/schließt die Bank?**
bank open/close?	*vahn <u>erf</u> • nuht/shleest dee bahnk*
I'd like to change	**Ich möchte Dollar/Pfund in Euro**
dollars/pounds	**wechseln.**
into euros.	*eekh <u>mehrkh</u> • tuh doh • lahr/pfoont*
	ihn <u>oy</u> • roh vehkh • zuhln
I'd like to cash	**Ich möchte Reiseschecks einlösen.**
traveler's checks	*eekh <u>mehrkh</u> • tuh <u>ric</u> • zuh • sheliks*
[cheques].	*ien • <u>ler</u> • zuhn*

AT THE BANK

I'd like to change	**Ich möchte Geld wechseln.**
money/get a cash	*eekh <u>mehrkh</u> • tuh gehlt <u>vehkh</u> • zuhln*
advance.	
What's the exchange	**Was ist der Wechselkurs/die Gebühr?**
rate/fee?	*vahs ihst dehr <u>vehkh</u> • zuhl • koors/dee*
	guh • <u>bewr</u>
I think there's	**Ich glaube, hier stimmt etwas nicht.**
a mistake.	*eekh <u>glow</u> • buh heer shtihmt <u>eht</u> • vahs*
	neekht

I lost my traveler's cheques.	**Ich habe meine Reiseschecks verloren.**
	eekh hah • buh mie • nuh rie • zuh • shecks fehr • loh • ruhn
My card was stolen/doesn't work.	**Meine Karte wurde gestohlen/ funktioniert nicht.**
	mie • nuh kahr • tuh voor • duh guh • shtoh • luhn/foonk • tzyoh • neert neekht
My card was lost.	**Ich habe meine Karte verloren.**
	eek hah • buh mie • nuh kahr • tuh fehr • loh • ruhn
The ATM ate my card.	**Der Bankautomat hat meine Karte eingezogen.**
	dehr bahnk • ow • toh • maht haht mie • nuh kahr • tuh ien • geh • tsoh • ghun

---

YOU MAY SEE...

KARTE HIER EINFÜHREN	insert card here
ABBRECHEN	cancel
LÖSCHEN	clear
EINGEBEN	enter
PIN-NUMMER	PIN
ABHEBUNG	withdrawal
VOM GIROKONTO	from checking [current] account
VOM SPARKONTO	from savings account
QUITTUNG	receipt

The best rates for exchanging money will be found at banks. You can also change money at travel agencies, currency exchange offices and hotels, though the rate may not be as good. Traveler's checks are accepted at most banks (though banks are not required to accept them) and currency exchange offices, but a variable fee will be charged. Cash can be obtained from **Bankautomaten** (ATMs) with many international bank and credit cards. ATMs are multilingual, so English-language instructions can be selected. Remember to bring your passport when you want to change money.

YOU MAY SEE...

German currency is the **Euro €**, divided into 100 **Cent**.
Coins: 1, 2, 5, 10, 20, 50 **Cent**; €1, 2
Notes: €5, 10, 20, 50, 100, 200, 500

CONVERSATION

NEED TO KNOW

Hello!	**Hallo!**
	hah • loh
How are you?	**Wie geht es Ihnen?**
	vee geht ehs eehn • uhn
Fine, thanks.	**Gut, danke.**
	goot dahn • kuh
Excuse me!	**Entschuldigung!**
	ehnt • shool • dee • goong
Do you speak English?	**Sprechen Sie Englisch?**
	shpreh • khuhn zee ehn • gleesh
What's your name?	**Wie heißen Sie?**
	vee hie • suhn zee
My name is...	**Mein Name ist ...**
	mien nahm • uh ihst ...
Nice to meet you.	**Schön, Sie kennenzulernen.**
	shern zee keh • nehn • tsoo • lehr • nehn
Where are you from?	**Woher kommen Sie?**
	voh • hehr koh • muhn zee
I'm from the U.S./ U.K.	**Ich komme aus den USA/ Großbritannien.**
	eekh koh • muh ows dehn oo • ehs • ah/ grohs • bree • tah • nee • ehn
What do you do for a living?	**Was machen Sie beruflich?**
	vahs mah • khuhn zee beh • roof • likh
I work for...	**Ich arbeite für ...**
	eekh ahr • bie • tuh fewr ...
I'm a student.	**Ich bin Student.**
	eekh bihn shtoo • dehnt

I'm retired.	**Ich bin Rentner.**
	eekh been <u>rehnt</u>•nehr
Do you like…?	**Mögen Sie …?**
	<u>mer</u>•guhn zee …
Goodbye.	**Auf Wiedersehen.**
	owf <u>vee</u>•dehr•zehn
See you later.	**Bis bald.**
	bihs bahld

When addressing anyone but a very close friend, it is polite to use a title: **Herr** (Mr.), **Frau** (Miss/Ms./Mrs.) or **Herr Dr.** (Dr.), and to speak to him or her using **Sie**, the formal form of 'you', until you are asked to use the familiar **Du**.

LANGUAGE DIFFICULTIES

Do you speak English?	**Sprechen Sie Englisch?**
	shpreh•khehn zee <u>ehn</u>•gleesh
Does anyone here speak English?	**Spricht hier jemand Englisch?**
	shpreekht heer <u>yeh</u>•mahnt <u>ehn</u>•gleesh
I don't speak (much) German.	**Ich spreche kein (nicht viel) Deutsch.**
	eekh <u>shpreh</u>•khuh kien (neekht feel) doych
Can you speak more slowly, please?	**Können Sie bitte langsamer sprechen?**
	<u>ker</u>•nuhn zee <u>biht</u>•tuh <u>lahng</u>•sahm•ehr <u>shpreh</u>•khuhn
Can you repeat that, please?	**Können Sie das bitte wiederholen?**
	<u>ker</u>•nuhn zee dahs <u>biht</u>•tuh vee•dehr•<u>hoh</u>•luhn

Excuse me?	**Wie bitte?**
	vee <u>biht</u> • tuh
What was that?	**Was haben Sie gesagt?**
	vahs <u>hah</u> • buhn zee guh • <u>zahgt</u>
Can you spell it?	**Können Sie das buchstabieren?**
	<u>ker</u> • nuhn zee dahs book • shtah • <u>bee</u> • ruhn
Write it down, please.	**Bitte schreiben Sie es auf.**
	<u>biht</u> • tuh <u>shrie</u> • buhn zee ehs owf
Can you translate this into English for me?	**Können Sie das für mich ins Englische übersetzen?**
	<u>ker</u> • nuhn zee dahs fewr meekh ihns <u>ehn</u> • glee • shuh ew • behr • <u>zeh</u> • tsuhn
What does… mean?	**Was bedeutet …?**
	vahs beh • <u>doyt</u> • eht …
I understand.	**Ich verstehe.**
	eekh fehr • <u>shteh</u> • uh
I don't understand.	**Ich verstehe nicht.**
	eekh fehr • <u>shteh</u> • uh neekht
Do you understand?	**Verstehen Sie?**
	fehr • <u>shteh</u> • uhn zee

YOU MAY HEAR…

Ich spreche nur wenig Englisch.	I only speak a
eekh <u>shpreh</u> • khuh noor <u>veh</u> • neek ehn • gleesh	little English.
Ich spreche kein Englisch.	I don't speak
eekh <u>shpreh</u> • khuh kien <u>ehn</u> • gleesh	English.

MAKING FRIENDS

Hello!	**Hallo!**
	hah • loh
Good morning.	**Guten Morgen.**
	goo • tuhn mohr • guhn
Good afternoon.	**Guten Tag.**
	goo • tuhn tahk
Good evening.	**Guten Abend.**
	goo • tuhn ah • behnt
My name is...	**Mein Name ist ...**
	mien nahm • uh ihst ...
What's your name?	**Wie heißen Sie?**
	vee hie • sehn zee
I'd like to introduce you to...	**Ich möchte Sie gern ... vorstellen.**
	eekh merkh • tuh zee gehrn ...
	fohr • shteh • luhn
Pleased to meet you.	**Angenehm.**
	ahn • guh • nehm
How are you?	**Wie geht es Ihnen?**
	vee geht ehs eehn • uhn
Fine, thanks. And you?	**Gut, danke. Und Ihnen?**
	goot dahn • kuh oont cehn • uhn

In Germany, it's polite to shake hands, both when you meet and say goodbye. Relatives and close friends may hug or kiss cheeks.

TRAVEL TALK

I'm here on business.	**Ich bin geschäftlich hier.** *eekh bihn guh • shehft • leekh heer*
I'm here on vacation.	**Ich mache hier Urlaub.** *eekh mahkh • uh heer oor • lowb*
I'm studying here.	**Ich bin zum Studieren hier.** *eekh bihn tsoom shtoo • dee • ruhn heer*
I'm staying for...	**Ich bleibe ...** *eekh blie • buh ...*
I've been here...	**Ich bin seit ... hier.** *eekh been ziet ... heer*
a day	**einem Tag** *ien • uhm tahk*
a week	**einer Woche** *ien • uhr voh • khuh*
a month	**einem Monat** *ien • uhm moh • naht*
Where are you from?	**Woher kommen Sie?** *voh • hehr koh • muhn zee*
I'm from...	**Ich komme aus ...** *eekh koh • muh ows ...*

For Numbers, see page 22.

PERSONAL

Who are you with?	**Mit wem sind Sie hier?** *miht vehm zihnt zee heer*
I'm here alone.	**Ich bin allein hier.** *eekh bihn ah • lien heer*
How old are you?	**Wie alt sind Sie?** *vee ahlt zihnt zee*

I'm...	**Ich bin ...**
	eekh bihn ...
I'm with...	**Ich bin mit ... hier.**
	eekh been miht ... heer
my husband/wife	**meinem Mann/meiner Frau**
	mie • nuhm mahn/mie • nuhr frow
my boyfriend/	**meinem Freund/meiner Freundin**
my girlfriend	*mie • nuhm froynt/mie • nuhr froyn • dihn*
my friend	**meinem Freund**
	mie • nuhm froynt
my friends	**meinen Freunden**
	mie • nuhn froyn • duhn
my colleague	**meinem Kollegen**
	mie • nuhm koh • leh • guhn
my colleagues	**meinen Kollegen**
	mie • nuhn koh • leh • guhn
When's your birthday?	**Wann haben Sie Geburtstag?**
	vahn hah • buhn zee guh • boorts • tahk
Are you married?	**Sind Sie verheiratet?**
	zihnt zee fehr • hie • rah • tuht
I'm...	**Ich bin ...**
	eekh bihn ...
single/in a relationship	**ledig/in einer Beziehung**
	leh • deek/ihn ien • uhr beh • tsee • oong
engaged	**verlobt**
	fehr • lohbt
married	**verheiratet**
	fehr • hie • rah • tuht
divorced	**geschieden**
	geh • shee • dehn
separated	**getrennt lebend**
	geh • trehnt leh • buhnd
widowed	**verwitwet**
	fehr • viht • veht

Do you have children/ grandchildren?	**Haben Sie Kinder/Enkelkinder?** <u>hah</u> • buhn zee <u>kihn</u> • dehr/ <u>ehn</u> • kehl • kihn • dehr

For Numbers, see page 22.

WORK & SCHOOL

What are you studying?	**Was studieren Sie?** vahs shtoo • <u>dee</u> • ruhn zee
I'm studying German.	**Ich studiere Deutsch.** eekh shtoo • <u>dee</u> • ruh doych
What do you do for a living?	**Was machen Sie beruflich?** vahs <u>mah</u> • khuhn zee beh • <u>roof</u> • leekh
I...	**Ich ...** eekh ...
work full-time/ part-time	**arbeite Vollzeit/Teilzeit** <u>ahr</u> • bie • tuh <u>fohl</u> • tsiet/<u>tiel</u> • tsiet
do freelance work	**bin Freiberufler** bihn <u>frie</u> • beh • roo • flehr
am a consultant	**bin Berater** bihn beh • <u>rah</u> • tehr
am unemployed	**bin arbeitslos** bihn <u>ahr</u> • biets • lohs
work at home	**arbeite zu Hause** <u>ahr</u> • bie • tuh tsoo <u>how</u> • zuh
Who do you work for?	**Für wen arbeiten Sie?** fewr vehn <u>ahr</u> • bie • tuhn zee
I work for...	**Ich arbeite für ...** eekh <u>ahr</u> • bie • tuh fewr ...
Here's my business card.	**Hier ist meine Visitenkarte.** heer ihst <u>mie</u> • nuh vih • <u>zee</u> • tuhn • kahr • tuh

For Communications, see page 86.

WEATHER

What's the forecast?	**Wie ist die Wettervorhersage?**
	vee ihst dee
	<u>veh</u> • tehr • fohr • hehr • zahg • uh
What beautiful/ terrible weather!	**Was für ein schönes/schlechtes Wetter!**
	vahs fewr ien <u>sher</u> • nuhs/<u>shlehkht</u> • uhs
	<u>veh</u> • tehr
It's…	**Es ist …**
	ehs ihst …
cool/warm	**kühl/warm**
	kewl/vahrm
cold/hot	**kalt/heiß**
	kahlt/hies
rainy/sunny	**regnerisch/sonnig**
	<u>rehg</u> • nuh • reesh/<u>zoh</u> • neek
There is snow/ice.	**Es gibt Schnee/Eis.**
	ehs gihbt shneh/ies
Do I need a jacket/ an umbrella?	**Brauche ich eine Jacke/einen Regenschirm?**
	<u>brow</u> • khuh eekh <u>ien</u> • uh <u>yah</u> • kuh/
	<u>ien</u> • uhn <u>reh</u> • guhn • sheerm

For Days, see page 26.

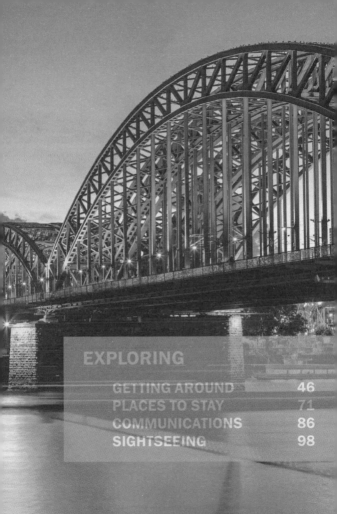

EXPLORING

NEED TO KNOW

How do I get to town?	**Wie komme ich in die Stadt?**
	vee koh • muh eekh ihn dee shtaht
Where's...?	**Wo ist ...?**
	voh ihst ...
the airport	**der Flughafen**
	dehr flook • hah • fuhn
the train [railway] station	**der Bahnhof**
	dehr bahn • hohf
the bus station	**die Bushaltestelle**
	dee boos • hahl • tuh • shteh • luh
the subway [underground] station	**die U-Bahn-Haltestelle**
	dee oo • bahn • hahl • tuh • shteh • luh
Is it far from here?	**Wie weit ist es?**
	vee viet ihst ehs
Where do I buy a ticket?	**Wo kann ich eine Fahrkarte kaufen?**
	voh kahn eekh ie • nuh fahr • kahr • tuh kow • fuhn

A one-way/ return ticket to...	**Ein Einzelticket/Eine Fahrkarte für Hin und Rückfahrt nach ...** *ien • ien • tsehl • tee • kuht/ie • nuh <u>fahr</u> • kahr • tuh fewr hihn oond <u>rewk</u> • fahrt nahkh...*
How much?	**Wie viel kostet es?** *vee feel <u>kohs</u> • tuhl ehs*
Which gate/line?	**Welches Gate/Linie?** *<u>vehl</u> • khehs <u>geht</u>/leen • yah*
Which platform?	**Welcher Bahnsteig?** *<u>vehl</u> • khehr <u>bahn</u> • shtieg*
Where can I get a taxi?	**Wo finde ich ein Taxi?** *voh <u>fihn</u> • duh eekh ien <u>tahk</u> • see*
Take me to this address, please.	**Bitte fahren Sie mich zu dieser Adresse.** *biht • tuh <u>fah</u> • ruhn zee meekh tsoo <u>dee</u> • zehr ah • <u>dreh</u> • suh*
Can I have a map, please?	**Können Sie mir bitte einen Stadtplan geben?** *<u>ker</u> • nuhn zee mihr <u>biht</u> • tuh ien • uhn <u>shtaht</u> • plahn gch • behn*

TICKETS

When's...to Berlin?	**Wann geht ... nach Berlin?** *vahn geht ... nahkh behr • <u>leen</u>*
the (first) bus	**der (erste) Bus** *dehr (<u>ehr</u> • stuh) boos*
the (next) flight	**der (nächste) Flug** *dehr (<u>nehks</u> • tuh) floog*
the (last) train	**der (letzte) Zug** *dehr (<u>lehts</u> • tuh) tsoog*

Where do I buy...?	**Wo kaufe ich ...?**
	voh kow • fuh eekh ...
One/two airline ticket(s), please.	**Ein/Zwei Ticket(s), bitte.**
	ien/tsvie tee • kuht(s) biht • tuh
One/two (bus/train/ subway) ticket(s), please.	**Ein/Zwei Fahrkarte(n), bitte.**
	ien/tsvie fahr • kahr • tuh(n) biht • tuh
For today/tomorrow.	**Für heute/morgen.**
	fewr hoy • tuh/mohr • guhn
A...(airline) ticket.	**Ein ... Ticket.**
	ien ... tee • kuht
one-way	**einfaches**
	ien • fah • khuhs
return trip	**Hin- und Rückflug-**
	hihn oont rewk • floog
first class	**Erste-Klasse-**
	ehr • stuh • klah • suh
business class	**Business-Class-**
	bihz • nehs • klahs
economy class	**Economy-Class-**
	eh • koh • noh • mee • klahs
A...(bus/train/ subway) ticket.	**Eine ...**
	ie • nuh ...
one-way	**Einzelfahrkarte**
	ien • zuhl • fahr • karh • tuh
return trip	**Hin- und Rückfahrkarte**
	hihn oont rewk • fahr • kahr • tuh
first class	**Erste-Klasse-Fahrkarte**
	ehr • stuh • klah • suh • fahr • karh • tuh
How much?	**Wie viel kostet es?**
	vee feel kohs • tuht ehs
Can I buy a ticket on the bus/train?	**Kann ich im Bus/Zug eine Fahrkarte kaufen?**
	kahn eekh ihm boos/tsoog ie • nuh fahr • kahr • tuh kow • fuhn

I have an airline/ a train e-ticket.	**Ich habe ein E-Ticket/Online-Ticket.**
	eekh hah • buh ien ay • tee • keht/ ohn • lien • tee • keht
Is there a discount for...?	**Gibt es eine Ermäßigung für ...?**
	gihpt ehs ie • nuh ehr • meh • see • goong fewr ...
children	**Kinder**
	kihn • dehr
students	**Studenten**
	shtoo • dehn • tuhn
senior citizens	**Rentner**
	rehnt • nehr
tourists	**Touristen**
	too • rih • stuhn
The express/local bus/train, please.	**Den Express-/Nahverkehrs-Bus/Zug, bitte.**
	dehn ehks • prehs • / nah • fuhr • kehrs • boos/tsoog biht • tuh
Do I have to stamp the ticket before boarding?	**Muss ich das Ticket vor dem Einsteigen entwerten?**
	moos eekh dahs tihk • khet fohr dehm ayn • shtayg • uhn ehnt • vehr • thun
How long is this ticket valid?	**Wie lange ist das Ticket gültig?**
	vee lahng • uh ihst dahs tihk • khet gewl • teekh
Can I return on the same ticket?	**Kann ich mit demselben Ticket zurückfahren?**
	kahn eekh miht dehm • sehl • bhun tihk • khet tsoo • rewkh • fah • ruhn
I'd like to... my reservation.	**Ich möchte meine Reservierung ...**
	eekh merkh • tuh mie • nuh reh • zehr • vee • roong ...
cancel	**stornieren**
	shtohr • nee • ruhn

change	**ändern**
	ehn • dehrn
confirm	**bestätigen**
	beh • shtay • tee • guhn

For Days, see page 26.

AIRPORT TRANSFER

How much is a taxi to the airport?	**Was kostet ein Taxi zum Flughafen?**
	vahs kohs • tuht ien tahk • see tsoom flook • hah • fuhn
To…Airport, please.	**Zum Flughafen …, bitte.**
	tsoom flook • hah • fuhn … biht • tuh
My airline is…	**Meine Fluggesellschaft ist …**
	mie • nuh floo • geh • zehl • shahft ihst …
My flight leaves at…	**Mein Flug geht um …**
	mien floog geht oom …
I'm in a rush.	**Ich habe es eilig.**
	eekh hah • buh ehs ie • leek
Can you take an alternate route?	**Können Sie eine andere Strecke fahren?**
	ker • nuhn zee ie • nuh ahn • deh • ruh shtreh • kuh fah • ruhn
Can you drive faster/slower?	**Können Sie schneller/langsamer fahren?**
	ker • nuhn zee shneh • lehr/ lahng • sah • mehr fah • ruhn

For Time, see page 25.

YOU MAY HEAR...

**Mit welcher Fluggesellschaft
fliegen Sie?**
*meet <u>vehlkh</u> • ehr <u>floog</u> • geh • sehl • shahft
flee • gehn zee*

Which airline are
you flying?

Inland oder international?
*<u>ihn</u> • <u>lahnt oh</u> • dehr
ihn • tuhr • nah • syoh • <u>nahl</u>*

Domestic or
international?

Welcher Terminal?
<u>vehlkh</u> • ehr tehr • mee • <u>nahl</u>

What terminal?

YOU MAY SEE...

ANKUNFT	arrivals
ABFLUG	departures
GEPÄCKAUSGABE	baggage claim
INLANDSFLÜGE	domestic flights
INTERNATIONALE FLÜGE	international flights
CHECK-IN	check-in
E-TICKET CHECK-IN	e-ticket check-in
ABFLUG-GATES	departure gates

CHECKING IN

Where's check-in?	**Wo ist das Check-in?** *voh ihst dahs <u>tshehk</u> • in*
My name is...	**Mein Name ist ...** *mien <u>nahm</u> • uh ihst ...*

I'm going to…	**Ich reise nach …**
	eekh riez • uh nahkh …
I have…	**Ich habe …**
	eekh hahb • uh …
one suitcase	**einen Koffer**
	ien • uhn kohf • fehr
two suitcases	**zwei Koffer**
	tsvie kohf • fehr
one piece of hand luggage	**ein Handgepäckstück**
	ien hahnd • guh • pehk • shtewk
How much luggage is allowed?	**Wie viel Gepäck ist erlaubt?**
	vee feel guh • pehk ihst ehr • lowbt
Is that pounds or kilos?	**Sind das Pfund oder Kilo?**
	zihnt dahs pfoont oh • duhr kee • loh
Which terminal?	**Welcher Terminal?**
	vehlkh • ehr tehr • mee • nahl
Which gate?	**Welches Gate?**
	vehlkh • uhs geht
I'd like a window/ an aisle seat.	**Ich möchte gern einen Fensterplatz/ Platz am Gang.**
	eekh merkht • uh gehrn ien • uhn fehnst • ehr • plahts/plahts ahm gahng
When do we leave/arrive?	**Wann ist der Abflug/die Ankunft?**
	vahn ihst dehr ahp • floog/dee ahn • kuhnft
Is the flight delayed?	**Hat der Flug Verspätung?**
	haht dehr floog fehr • shpeh • toong
How late?	**Wie viel?**
	vee feel

LUGGAGE

Where is/are…?	**Wo ist/sind …?**
	voh ihst/zihnt …

the luggage trolleys	**die Gepäckwagen** *dee guh • pehk • vah • guhn*
the luggage lockers	**die Gepäckschließfächer** *dee guh • pehk • shlees • fehkh • ehr*

YOU MAY HEAR...

Der Nächste, bitte!
dehr nehkhst • uh biht • tuh

Next, please!

Ihren Reisepass/Ihr Ticket, bitte.
eehr • uhn riez • uh • pahs/eehr tih • kuht biht • tuh

Your passport/ ticket, please.

Geben Sie Gepäck auf?
gehb • ehn zee guh • pehk owf

Are you checking in any luggage?

Das ist zu groß für Handgepäck.
dahs ihst tsoo grohs fuehr hahnd • guh • pehk

That's too large for a carry-on [piece of hand luggage].

Haben Sie diese Taschen selbst gepackt?
hah • buhn zee dees • uh tahsh • uhn sehlbst guh • pahkt

Did you pack these bags yourself?

Hat Ihnen jemand etwas mitgegeben?
haht eehn • uhn yeh • mahnd eht • vahs miht • guh • geh • buhn

Did anyone give you anything to carry?

Leeren Sie Ihre Taschen.
lehr • uhn zee eehr • uh tahsh • uhn

Empty your pockets.

Ziehen Sie Ihre Schuhe aus.
tsee • uhn zee eehr • uh shoo • uh ows

Take off your shoes.

Wir beginnen jetzt mit dem Einsteigen...
weer beh • gihn • nuhn yehtst miht dehm ayn • shtayg • uhn ...

We are now boarding...

the baggage claim	**die Gepäckausgabe**
	dee guh • pehk • ows • gahb • uh
My luggage has been lost/stolen.	**Mein Gepäck ist weg/wurde gestohlen.**
	mien guh • pehk ihst vehk/voor • duh guh • shtohl • uhn
My suitcase is damaged.	**Mein Koffer wurde beschädigt.**
	mien kohf • fehr voord • uh buh • shehd • eekht

FINDING YOUR WAY

Where is/are...?	**Wo ist/sind ...?**
	voh ihst/zihnt ...
the currency exchange	**die Wechselstube**
	dee vehkh • zuhl • shtoo • buh
the car hire	**die Autovermietung**
	dee ow • toh • fehr • meet • oong
the exit	**der Ausgang**
	dehr ows • gahng
the taxis	**die Taxis**
	dee tahks • ees
Is there a...into town?	**Gibt es ... in die Stadt?**
	gihbt ehs ... ihn dee shtadt
bus	**einen Bus**
	ien • uhn boos
train	**einen Zug**
	ien • uhn tsoog
subway [underground]	**eine U-Bahn**
	ien • uh oo • bahn

For Asking Directions, see page 66.

TRAIN

Where's the train [railway] station?	**Wo ist der Bahnhof?** *voh ihst dehr bahn • hohf*
How far is it?	**Wie weit ist es?** *vee viet ihst ehs*
Where is/are...?	**Wo ist/sind ...?** *voh ihst/zihnt ...*
the ticket office	**der Fahrkartenschalter** *dehr fahr • kahrt • uhn • shahl • tehr*
the information desk	**die Information** *dee ihn • fohrm • ah • syohn*
the luggage lockers	**die Gepäckschließfächer** *dee guh • pehk • shlees • fehkh • ehr*
the platforms	**die Bahnsteige** *dee bahn • shtieg • uh*
Can I have a schedule [timetable]?	**Kann ich einen Fahrplan haben?** *kahn eehk ien • uhn fahr • plahn hah • buhn*
How long is the trip?	**Wie lange dauert die Fahrt?** *vee lahng • uh dow • ehrt dee fahrt*
Is it a direct train?	**Ist das eine direkte Zugverbindung?** *ihst dahs ien • uh dee • rehkt tsoog • ver • bind • ungh*

YOU MAY SEE...

BAHNSTEIGE	platforms
INFORMATION	information
RESERVIERUNGEN	reservations
WARTERAUM	waiting room
ANKUNFT	arrivals
ABFAHRT	departures

German trains are fast, comfortable and reliable.
Train travel in Germany is a highly recommended alternative
to driving. The **Deutsche Bahn AG** is the national railway of
Germany. It offers many domestic and international routes.
Tickets can be purchased at the station or through a travel
agent. Buy your tickets in advance to get the cheapest fare
and to guarantee seating. Many reduced-fare options are
available; visit the **Deutsche Bahn AG** website or speak to a
travel agent for more information.

Do I have to change trains?	**Muss ich umsteigen?**
	moos eekh <u>oom</u> • shtieg • uhn
Is the train on time?	**Ist der Zug pünktlich?**
	ihst dehr tsoog <u>pewnkt</u> • leekh

For Numbers, see page 22.

DEPARTURES

Which track [platform] to…?	**Von welchem Bahnsteig fährt der Zug nach …?** *fohn vehlkh • ehm bahn • shtieg fehrt dehr tsoog nahkh …*
Is this the track [platform]/train to…?	**Ist das der Bahnsteig/Zug nach …?** *ihst dahs dehr bahn • shtieg/tsoog nahkh …*
Where is platform…?	**Wo ist Bahnsteig …?** *voh ihst bahn • shtieg …*
Where do I change for…?	**Wo steige ich um nach …?** *voh shtieg • uh eekh oom nahkh …*

YOU MAY HEAR…

Bitte einsteigen! *biht • tuh ien • shtieg • uhn*	All aboard!
Die Fahrkarten, bitte. *dee fahr • kahr • tuhn biht • tuh*	Tickets, please.
Sie müssen in … umsteigen. *zee mews • uhn ihn … oom • shtieg • uhn*	You have to change at…
Nächster Halt … Hauptbahnhof. *nehkh • stehr hahlt … howpt • bahn • hohf*	Next stop…

ON BOARD

Can I sit here?	**Kann ich mich hier hinsetzen?** *kahn eekh meekh heer hihn • seht • suhn*
Can I open the window?	**Kann ich das Fenster öffnen?** *kahn eekh dahs fehn • stehr erf • nuhn*

Is this seat available?	**Ist der Platz frei?**
	ihst dehr plahts frie
That's my seat.	**Das ist mein Platz.**
	dahs ihst mien plahts
Here's my reservation.	**Hier ist meine Reservierung.**
	heer ihst mien • uh reh • sehr • veer • roong

BUS

Where's the bus station?	**Wo ist die Bushaltestelle?**
	voh ihst dee boos • hahlt • uh • shtehl • uh
How far is it?	**Wie weit ist es?**
	vee viet ihst ehs
How do I get to…?	**Wie komme ich nach …?**
	vee kohm • uh eekh nahk…
Is this the bus to…?	**Ist das der Bus nach …?**
	ihst dahs dehr boos nahkh…
Can you tell me when to get off?	**Können Sie mir sagen, wann ich aussteigen muss?**
	kerhn • uhn zee meer zahg • uhn vahn eekh ows • shtieg • uhn moos

---

Bus and tram stops are marked by a green **H** for **Haltestelle** (stop). Larger cities, such as Berlin, Munich and Hamburg, offer 24-hour service. Service is limited on holidays and weekends.

In large German cities, the same ticket or pass can be used for the bus, subway, tram and above-ground train systems. Purchase tickets from the machines at bus stops or subway/tram stations. Check with a local travel agency or tourist information office about special discount tickets and offers.

Do I have to change buses?	**Muss ich umsteigen?**
	moos eekh <u>oom</u> • shtieg • uhn
Stop here, please!	**Bitte halten Sie hier!**
	<u>biht</u> • tuh <u>hahlt</u> • uhn zee heer

For Tickets, see page 47.

YOU MAY SEE...   👁

BUSHALTESTELLE	bus stop
STOPP-TASTE	request stop
EINGANG/AUSGANG	enter/exit
FAHRSCHEIN ENTWERTEN	validate your ticket

METRO

Where's the U-Bahn [underground] station?	**Wo ist die U-Bahn-Haltestelle?**
	voh ihst dee <u>oo</u> • bahn • <u>halt</u> • uh • shtehl • uh
A map, please.	**Eine Übersichtskarte, bitte.**
	<u>ien</u> • nuh <u>ew</u> • behr • zehkhts • <u>kahr</u> • tuh <u>biht</u> • tuh
Which line for...?	**Welche Linie fährt nach ...?**
	<u>vehlkh</u> • uh <u>lihn</u> • ee • uh fehrt nahkh ...
Which direction?	**Welche Richtung?**
	<u>vehlkh</u> • uh <u>reekh</u> • toong
Do I have to transfer [change]?	**Muss ich umsteigen?**
	moos eekh oom • <u>shtieg</u> • uhn
Is this the U-Bahn [train] to...?	**Ist das die U-Bahn nach ...?**
	ihst dahs dee <u>oo</u> • bahn nahkh ...

YOU MAY SEE...

FAHRTZIEL	destination
EINZELFAHRT	one-trip ticket
TAGESKARTE	day pass
GRUPPENKARTE	group pass
WOCHENKARTE	weekly pass

How many stops to...?	**Wie viele Haltestellen sind es bis ...?** *vee <u>feel</u> • uh halt • uh • shtehl • uhn zihnt ehs bihs ...*
Where are we?	**Wo sind wir?** *voh zihnt veer*

For Tickets, see page 47.

BOAT & FERRY

When is the ferry to...?	**Wann geht die Fähre nach ...?** *vahn geht dee <u>fehr</u> • uh nahkh ...*
Can I take my car?	**Kann ich mein Auto mitnehmen?** *kahn eekh mien <u>ow</u> • toh <u>miht</u> • nehm • uhn*
What time is the next sailing?	**Wann fährt das nächste Schiff ab?** *vahn fehrt dahs nehkh • ste shihf ahb*
Can I book a seat/cabin?	**Kann ich einen Sitzplatz/eine Kabine reservieren?** *kahn eekh <u>ien</u> • uhn <u>sihts</u> • plahts/ien • uh kah • <u>bee</u> • nuh reh • sehr • <u>veer</u> • uhn*
How long is the crossing?	**Wie lange dauert die Überfahrt?** *vee <u>lahng</u> • uh dow • ehrt dee <u>ew</u> • behr • fahrt*

For Weather, see page 43.

YOU MAY SEE...

RETTUNGSBOOT	life boat
SCHWIMMWESTE	life jacket

Ferry service across the Baltic Sea is available between Germany and Denmark, Sweden, Finland and Norway, or across the North Sea to the U.K. Ferry service is also available across Lake Constance to Austria and Switzerland. Boat trips are a fun way to explore the many rivers and lakes throughout Germany. Ferry and boat trips can be arranged by contacting your travel agent or searching the internet.

TAXI

Where can I get a taxi?	**Wo finde ich ein Taxi?**
	voh fihnd • uh eekh ien tahk • see
Can you send a taxi?	**Können Sie ein Taxi schicken?**
	kern • nuhn zee ein tahk • see shihk • uhn
Do you have the number for a taxi?	**Haben Sie die Telefonnummer für ein Taxi?**
	hah • buhn zee dee tehl • uh • fohn • noom • ehr fewr ien tahk • see
I'd like a taxi now/ for tomorrow at...	**Ich brauche jetzt/für morgen um ... ein Taxi.**
	eekh browkh • uh yehtst/fewr mohrg • uhn oom ... ien tahk • see

Pick me up at...	**Holen Sie mich um ... ab.**
	hohl • uhn zee meekh oom ... ahp
I'm going...	**Ich möchte ...**
	eekh merkh • tuh ...
to this address	**zu dieser Adresse**
	tsoo deez • ehr ah • drehs • suh
to the airport	**zum Flughafen**
	tsoom floog • hah • fuhn
to the train station	**zum Bahnhof**
	tsoom bahn • hohf
I'm late.	**Ich bin spät dran.**
	eekh bihn shpayt drahn
Can you drive faster/slower?	**Können Sie schneller/langsamer fahren?**
	kern • nuhn zee shnehl • ehr/ lahng • sahm • ehr fahr • uhn
Stop here.	**Halten Sie hier an.**
	hahl • tuhn zee heer ahn
Wait here.	**Warten Sie hier.**
	vahrt • uhn zee heer
How much?	**Wie viel kostet es?**
	vee feel kohs • tuht ehs
You said it would cost...	**Sie sagten, es würde ... kosten.**
	zee zahg • tuhn ehs vewrd • uh ... kohs • tuhn

Keep the change. **Stimmt so.**
shtihmt zoh

The receipt, please. **Die Quittung, bitte.**
dee kviht • oong biht • tuh

YOU MAY HEAR...

Wohin?
voh • hihn
Where to?

Wie ist die Adresse?
wee ihst dee ah • drehs • uh
What's the address?

Es wird ein Nachtzuschlag/
Flughafenzuschlag berechnet.
ehs veerd ien nahkht • tsoo • shlahg/
floog • hahf • uhn • tsoo • shlahg
buh • rehkh • nuht
There's a nighttime/ airport surcharge.

You can catch a taxi at taxi stands, by calling to arrange for pick up, or by flagging down a passing available taxi. Taxi stands can be found at train stations, airports, large hotels and other popular areas in the city, such as shopping areas, parks and tourist destinations. Taxi service numbers can be found in the phone book or by asking your hotel concierge. All taxis are metered and will charge a base rate plus a rate per kilometer traveled. To tip the driver, round the fare up to the next euro or two, depending on the service.

BICYCLE & MOTORBIKE

I'd like to hire…	**Ich möchte gern … mieten.**
	eekh merkh • tuh gehrn … meet • uhn
a bicycle	**ein Fahrrad**
	ien fahr • raht
a moped	**ein Moped**
	ien moh • pehd
a motorbike	**ein Motorrad**
	ien moh • tohr • raht
How much per day/week?	**Wie viel pro Tag/Woche?**
	vee feel proh tahk/vohkh • uh
Can I have a helmet/lock?	**Kann ich einen Helm/ein Schloss haben?**
	kahn eekh ien • uhn hehlm/ien shlohs hah • buhn

CAR HIRE

Where's the car hire?	**Wo ist die Autovermietung?**
	voh ihst dee ow • toh • fehr • miet • oong
I'd like…	**Ich möchte …**
	eekh merkh • tuh …
a cheap/small car	**ein billiges/kleines Auto**
	ien bihl • lee • guhs/klien • uhs ow • toh
an automatic/ a manual car	**ein Auto mit Automatikschaltung/ Gangschaltung**
	ien ow • toh miht ow • toh • mah • teek • shahl • toong/ gahng • shahl • toong
air conditioning	**ein Auto mit Klimaanlage**
	ien ow • toh miht klee • mah • ahn • lah • guh
a car seat	**einen Kindersitz**
	ien • uhn kihnd • ehr • zihts

YOU MAY HEAR...

Haben Sie einen internationalen Führerschein?
hah • buhn zee ien • uhn
ihnt • ehr • nah • syoh • nahl • uhn
fewhr • uhr • shien

Do you have an international driver's license?

Ihren Reisepass, bitte.
eehr • uhn riez • uh • pahs biht • tuh

Your passport, please.

Möchten Sie eine Versicherung?
merkht • uhn zee ien • uh
fehr • seekh • ehr • roong

Do you want insurance?

Ich benötige eine Anzahlung. *eekh*
buh • nert • ee • guh ien • uh
ahn • tsah • loong

I'll need a deposit.

Bitte unterschreiben Sie hier.
biht • tuh oont • ehr • shrieb • uhn
zee heer

Sign here, please.

How much...?	**Wie viel kostet es ...?** *vee feel kohs • tuht ehs ...*
per day/week	**pro Tag/Woche** *proh tahk/vohkh • uh*
per kilometer	**pro Kilometer** *proh kee • loh • meh • tehr*
for unlimited mileage	**mit unbegrenzter Kilometerzahl** *miht oon • buh • grehnts • tuhr kee • loh • meh • tehr • tsahl*
with insurance	**mit Versicherung** *miht fehr • zeekh • ehr • oong*
Are there any discounts?	**Gibt es irgendwelche Ermäßigungen?** *gihpt ehs eer • guhnd • vehlkh • uh ehr • meh • see • goong • uhn*

FUEL STATION

Where's the fuel station?	**Wo ist die Tankstelle?** *voh ihst dee <u>tahnk</u>•shtehl•luh*
Fill it up, please.	**Bitte volltanken.** *<u>biht</u>•tuh <u>fohl</u>•tahnk•uhn*
...euros, please.	**... Euro, bitte. ...** *<u>oy</u>•roh biht•tuh*
I'll pay in cash/by credit card.	**Ich bezahle bar/mit Kreditkarte.** *eekh beht•<u>sahl</u>•uh bahr/miht kreh•<u>deet</u>•kahr•tuh*

YOU MAY SEE... 👁

BENZIN	gas [petrol]
BLEIFREI	unleaded
NORMAL	regular
SUPER	super
DIESEL	diesel

ASKING DIRECTIONS

Is this the way to...?	**Ist das der Weg nach ...?** *ihst dahs dehr vehg nahkh ...*
How far is it to...?	**Wie weit ist es bis ...?** *vee viet ihst ehs bihs ...*
Where's...?	**Wo ist ...?** *voh ihst ...*
Street	**die ... Straße** *dee ... <u>shtrahs</u>•suh*
this address	**diese Adresse** *<u>deez</u>•uh ah•<u>drehs</u>•uh*

the highway [motorway]	**die Autobahn** _dee • uh ow • toh • bahn_
Can you show me on the map?	**Können Sie mir das auf der Karte zeigen?** _kern • nuhn zee meer dahs owf dehr_ _kahrt • uh tsieg • uhn_

YOU MAY HEAR...

geradeaus _geh • rahd • uh • ows_	straight ahead
links _leenks_	left
rechts _rehkhts_	right
an der/um die Ecke _ahn dehr/oom dee eh • kuh_	on/around the corner
gegenüber _geh • guhn • ew • behr_	opposite
hinter _hihnt • ehr_	behind
neben _nehb • uhn_	next to
nach _nahkh_	after
nördlich/südlich _nerd • leekh/zewd • leekh_	north/south
östlich/westlich _erst • leekh/vehst • leekh_	east/west
an der Ampel _ahn dehr ahmp • ehl_	at the traffic light
an der Kreuzung _ahn dehr kroytz • oong_	at the intersection

YOU MAY SEE...

(50)	**HÖCHSTGESCHWINDIGKEIT**	maximum speed limit
	ÜBERHOLVERBOT	no passing
	VERBOT FÜR FAHRZEUGE ALLER ART	all vehicles prohibited
	EINBAHNSTRASSE	one-way street
	KEINE DURCHFAHRT	no entry
STOP	**STOPP**	stop
	VORFAHRT GEWÄHREN	yield

I'm lost.	**Ich habe mich verfahren.**
	eekh <u>hahb</u> • uh meekh fehr • <u>fahr</u> • uhn

PARKING

Can I park here?	**Kann ich hier parken?**
	kahn eekh heer <u>pahrk</u> • uhn
Where's...?	**Wo ist ...?**
	voh ihst ...
the parking garage	**das Parkhaus**
	dahs <u>pahrk</u> • hows
the parking lot [car park]	**der Parkplatz**
	dehr <u>pahrk</u> • plahts

(i)

Parking on the street is common in Germany; look for
the sign showing a white letter 'P' on a blue background. You
may see additional parking instructions located under the sign.
The parking sign with the meter symbol indicates that you
can park there for the amount of time shown (in hours - for
example, **2 Std.** means 2 hours). Ask your rental car company
for a parking disc when you pick up your car. Once parked, turn
the dial to indicate the time you parked and put the disc on
your dashboard where it is visible.

If you see a **mit Parkschein** sign you must buy a parking ticket
from a nearby machine and place it on your dashboard where
it is visible.

Parking lots and garages are other parking options. Most lots
and garages use a self-pay system. When entering, obtain the
time-stamped ticket from the machine. Use the machine near
the pedestrian entrance to pay for parking; insert your ticket
into the machine, pay the amount it displays and then remove
the validated ticket. Proceed to your car and insert that ticket
into the machine at the exit.

the parking meter	**die Parkuhr**
	dee <u>pahrk</u> • oor
How much…?	**Wie viel kostet es …?**
	vee feel <u>kohs</u> • tuht ehs …
per hour	**pro Stunde**
	proh <u>shtoond</u> • uh
per day	**pro Tag**
	proh tahk
for overnight	**über Nacht**
	<u>ew</u> • behr nahkht

BREAKDOWN & REPAIR

Where's the garage?	**Wo ist die Autowerkstatt?**
	voh ihst dee ow • toh • <u>vehrk</u> • shtaht
My car broke down/ won't start.	**Mein Auto ist kaputt/springt nicht an.**
	mien <u>ow</u> • toh ihst <u>kah</u> • poot/shprihngt neekht ahn
Can you fix it (today)?	**Können Sie es (heute) reparieren?**
	<u>kern</u> • nuhn zee ehs (<u>hoy</u> • tuh) reh • pah • <u>reer</u> • uhn
When will it be ready?	**Wann wird es fertig sein?**
	vahn wirt ehs <u>fehr</u> • teekh zien
How much?	**Wie viel kostet es?**
	vee feel <u>kohs</u> • tuht ehs
I have a puncture/ flat tyre (tire).	**Ich habe eine Reifenpanne.**
	eekh hah • buh ien • uh rie • fehn • pahn • nuh

ACCIDENTS

There was an accident.	**Es hat einen Unfall gegeben.** *ehs haht <u>ien</u> • uhn <u>oon</u> • fahl guh • <u>geh</u> • buhn*
Call an ambulance/ the police.	**Rufen Sie einen Krankenwagen/die Polizei.**
	<u>roof</u> • uhn zee <u>ien</u> • uhn <u>krahnk</u> • uhn • vahg • uhn/dee poh • lee • <u>tsie</u>

PLACES TO STAY

NEED TO KNOW

Can you recommend a hotel?	**Können Sie ein Hotel empfehlen?**
	ker • nuhn zee ien hoh • tehl ehm • pfeh • luhn
I have a reservation.	**Ich habe eine Reservierung.**
	eekh hahb • uh ien • uh rehz • ehr • veer • oong
My name is…	**Mein Name ist …**
	mien nahm • uh ihst …
Do you have a room…?	**Haben Sie ein Zimmer …?**
	hah • buhn zee ien tsihm • mehr …
for one person/ two people	**für eine Person/zwei Personen**
	fewr ien • uh pehr • sohn/tsvie pehr • sohn • uhn
with a bathroom	**mit Bad**
	miht bahd
with air conditioning	**mit Klimaanlage**
	miht kleem • uh • ahn • lahg • uh
For…	**Für …**
	fewr …
tonight	**heute Nacht**
	hoy • tuh nahkht
two nights	**zwei Nächte**
	tsvie nehkht • uh
one week	**eine Woche**
	ien • uh vohkh • uh
How much?	**Wie viel kostet es?**
	vee feel kohs • tuht ehs

Is there anything cheaper?	**Gibt es etwas Billigeres?** *gihpt ehs eht • vahs bihl • lee • geh • ruhs*
When's check-out?	**Wann ist der Check-out?** *vahn ihst dehr tshehk • owt*
Can I leave this in the safe?	**Kann ich das im Safe lassen?** *kahn eekh dahs ihm sehf lahs • suhn*
Can I leave my bags?	**Kann ich meine Taschen hierlassen?** *kahn eekh mien • uh tahsh • uhn heer • lahs • suhn*
Can I have my bill/a receipt?	**Kann ich meine Rechnung/eine Quittung haben?** *kahn eekh mien • uh rehkh • noong/ ien • uh kveet • oong hah • buhn*
I'll pay in cash/by credit card.	**Ich bezahle bar/mit Kreditkarte.** *eekh beht • sahl • uh bahr/miht kreh • deet • kahr • tuh*

SOMEWHERE TO STAY

Can you recommend…?	**Können Sie … empfehlen?** *kern • uhn zee … ehm • pfeh • luhn*
a hotel	**ein Hotel** *ien hoh • tehl*
a hostel	**eine Jugendherberge** *ien • uh yoog • uhnd • hehr • behr • guh*

If you didn't reserve accommodation before your trip, visit the local **Touristeninformationsbüro** (tourist information office) for recommendations on places to stay.

a campsite	**einen Campingplatz**
	ien • uhn <u>kahmp</u> • eeng • plahts
a bed and	**eine Pension**
breakfast	_<u>ien</u> • uh pehn • <u>syohn</u>_
What is near it?	**Was ist in der Nähe davon?**
	vahs ihst ihn dehr <u>neh</u> • uh dah • <u>fohn</u>
How do I get there?	**Wie komme ich dorthin?**
	vee <u>kohm</u> • uh eekh dohrt • <u>hihn</u>

AT THE HOTEL

I have a reservation.	**Ich habe eine Reservierung.**
	eekh <u>hahb</u> • uh <u>ien</u> • uh
	rehz • <u>ehr</u> • veer • oong
My name is…	**Mein Name ist …**
	mien <u>nahm</u> • uh ihst …
Do you have	**Haben Sie ein Zimmer …?**
a room…?	_hah • buhn zee ien <u>tsihm</u> • mehr …_
with a bathroom	**mit Bad/Dusche**
[toilet]/shower	_miht bahd/<u>doo</u> • shuh_
with air	**mit Klimaanlage**
conditioning	_miht <u>kleem</u> • uh • ahn • lah • guh_
that's smoking/	**für Raucher/Nichtraucher**
non-smoking	_fewr <u>rowkh</u> • ehr/<u>neekht</u> • rowkh • ehr_
For…	**Für …**
	fewr …
tonight	**heute Nacht**
	<u>hoyt</u> • uh nahkht
two nights	**zwei Nächte**
	tsvie <u>nehkht</u> • uh
a week	**eine Woche**
	<u>ien</u> • uh <u>vohkh</u> • uh
Do you have…?	**Haben Sie …?**
	hah • buhn zee …

> **YOU MAY HEAR...**
>
> **Ihren Reisepass/Ihre Kreditkarte, bitte.** Your passport /
> _eehr • uhn riez • uh • pahs/eehr • uh_ credit
> _kreh • deet • kahrt • uh biht • tuh_ card, please.
> **Bitte füllen Sie dieses Formular aus.** Fill out this form,
> _biht • tuh fewl • uhn zee deez • uhs_ please.
> _fohr • moo • lahr ows_
> **Bitte unterschreiben Sie hier.** Sign here,
> _biht • tuh oon • tehr • shrieb • uhn zee heer_ please.

a computer	**einen Computer**
	ien • uhn kohm • pjoot • ehr
an elevator [a lift]	**einen Fahrstuhl**
	ien • uhn fahr • shtoohl
(wireless) internet	**(wireless) Internetanschluss**
service	_(wier • luhs) ihnt • ehr • neht • ahn • shloos_
room service	**Zimmerservice**
	tsihm • mehr • sehr • vees
a pool	**einen Pool**
	ien • uhn pool
a gym	**einen Fitnessraum**
	ien • uhn fiht • nehs • rowm
I need...	**Ich brauche ...**
	eekh browkh • uh ...
an extra bed	**ein zusätzliches Bett**
	ien tsoo • zehts • leeks • uhs beht
a cot	**ein Kinderbett**
	ien kihnd • ehr • beht
a crib	**ein Gitterbett**
	ien giht • tehr • beht

For Numbers, see page 22.

ⓘ

Travelers have numerous accommodation options in Germany, from budget to luxury. A **Pension** (bed and breakfast) provides opportunities to experience life in a German home. **Jugendherbergen** (youth hostels) are also available, catering to travelers of all ages. **Urlaub auf dem Bauernhof** (farm stay) is a great way to see the countryside and enjoy rural Germany. In some areas, you may be able to find **Modernisierte Schlossunterkünfte**, old castles that have been converted into beautiful accommodations. **Ferienwohnungen** (vacation apartments) and **Ferienhäuser** (holiday homes) allow travelers to rent fully equipped apartments and villas throughout Germany. All options can be booked with travel agents, tour companies or on the internet.

PRICE

How much per night/week?	**Wie viel kostet es pro Nacht/Woche?** *vee feel <u>kohs</u> • tuht ehs proh nahkht/ <u>vohk</u> • uh*
Does that include breakfast/sales tax [VAT]?	**Beinhaltet der Preis ein Frühstück/ Mehrwertsteuer?** *beh • <u>ien</u> • hahlt • uht dehr pries ien <u>frewh</u> • shtewkh/<u>mehr</u> • wehrt • shtoy • ehr*
Are there any discounts?	**Gibt es irgendwelche Ermäßigungen?** *gihpt ehs <u>eer</u> • guhnd • vehlkh • uh ehr • <u>meh</u> • see • goong • uhn*

PREFERENCES

Can I see the room?	**Kann ich das Zimmer sehen?** *kahn eekh dahs <u>tsihm</u> • mehr <u>zeh</u> • uhn*

I'd like a…room.	**Ich möchte ein … Zimmer.**
	eekh merkh • tuh ien … tsihm • muhr
better	**besseres**
	behs • sehr • uhs
bigger	**größeres**
	grers • ehr • uhs
cheaper	**billigeres**
	bihl • lee • gehr • uhs
quieter	**ruhigeres**
	roo • ee • gehr • uhs
I'll take it.	**Ich nehme es.**
	eekh nehm • uh ehs
No, I won't take it.	**Nein, ich nehme es nicht.**
	nien eekh nehm • uh ehs neekht

QUESTIONS

Where's…?	**Wo ist …?**
	voh ihhst …
the bar	**die Bar**
	dee bahr
the bathroom [toilet]	**die Toilette**
	dee toy • leht
the elevator [lift]	**der Fahrstuhl**
	dehr fahr • shtoohl
Can I have…?	**Kann ich … haben?**
	kahn eekh … hah • buhn
a blanket	**eine Decke**
	ien • uh dehk • uh
an iron	**ein Bügeleisen**
	ien bew • guh • liez • ehn
the room key/ the key card	**den Zimmerschlüssel/die Schlüsselkarte**
	dehn tsihm • mehr • shlews • uhl/dee shlews • ehl • kahrt • uh

YOU MAY SEE...

DRÜCKEN/ZIEHEN	push/pull
TOILETTE	bathroom [toilet]
DUSCHE	shower
FAHRSTUHL	elevator [lift]
TREPPE	stairs
WÄSCHEREI	laundry
BITTE NICHT STÖREN	do not disturb
FEUERSCHUTZTÜR	fire door
NOTAUSGANG	(emergency) exit
WECKRUF	wake-up call

a pillow	**ein Kissen**	
	ien <u>kihs</u> • suhn	
soap	**Seife**	
	<u>zief</u> • uh	
toilet paper	**Toilettenpapier**	
	toy • <u>leht</u> • tuhn • pah • peer	
a towel	**ein Handtuch**	
	ien <u>hahnt</u> • tookh	
Do you have an	**Haben Sie hierfür einen Adapter?**	
	<u>hah</u> • buhn	
adapter for this?	*zee heer • <u>fewr</u> ien • uhn ah • <u>dahp</u> • tehr*	
How do I turn on	**Wie schalte ich das Licht an?**	
the lights?	*vee <u>shahlt</u> • uh eekh dahs leekht ahn*	
Can you wake	**Können Sie mich um ... wecken?**	
	<u>kern</u> • nuhn	
me at...?	*zee meekh oom ... <u>vehk</u> • uhn*	
Can I leave this in	**Kann ich das im Safe lassen?**	
the safe?	*kahn eekh dahs ihm sehf <u>lahs</u> • suhn*	

Can I have my things from the safe? **Kann ich meine Sachen aus dem Safe haben?**
kahn eekh mien • uh zahkh • uhn ows dehm sehf hah • buhn

Is there mail [post]/ a message for me? **Haben Sie Post/eine Nachricht für mich?**
hah • buhn zee pohst/ien • uh nahkh • reekht fewr meekh

Do you have a laundry service? **Bieten Sie einen Wäscheservice?**
bih • tuhn zee ien • uhn vehsh • eh • ser • vice

PROBLEMS

There's a problem. **Es gibt ein Problem.**
ehs gihbt ien prohb • lehm

I lost my key/my key card. **Ich habe meinen Schlüssel/meine Schlüsselkarte verloren.**
eekh hahb • uh mien • uhn shlews • uhl/ mien • uh shlews • ehl • kahrt • uh fehr • lohr • uhn

I'm locked out of the room. **Ich habe mich ausgesperrt.**
eekh hahb • uh meekh ows • guh • shpehrt

There's no hot water/toilet paper. **Ich habe kein heißes Wasser/ Toilettenpapier.**
eekh hahb • uh kien hies • suhs vahs • sehr/toy • leht • uhn • pah • peer

The room is dirty. **Das Zimmer ist schmutzig.**
dahs tsihm • mehr ihst shmoot • seek

There are bugs in the room. **Im Zimmer sind Insekten.**
ihm tsihm • mehr zihnt ihn • sehkt • uhn

Voltage is 220, and plugs are two-pronged. You may need a converter and/or an adapter for your appliances.

The...doesn't work.	**... funktioniert nicht.**
	... foonk • syoh • neert neekht
Can you fix...?	**Können Sie ... reparieren?**
	kern • nuhn zee ... reh • pah • reer • ruhn
the air conditioning	**die Klimaanlage**
	dee kleem • uh • ahn • lahg • uh
the fan	**den Ventilator**
	dehn vehn • tee • laht • ohr
the heat [heating]	**die Heizung**
	dee hiets • oong
the light	**das Licht**
	dahs leekht
the TV	**den Fernseher**
	dehn fehrn • seh • ehr
the toilet	**die Toilette**
	dee toy • leht • tuh
I'd like another room.	**Ich möchte gern ein anderes Zimmer.**
	eekh merkh • tuh gehrn ien ahn • dehr • uhs tsihm • mehr

ⓘ

At hotels, it is common to leave tips for services
provided. If you are happy with the housekeeping service,
leave a tip of a few euro per day for the housekeeper in your
room when you leave. The same applies for porters and
your concierge generally too – a few euros when a service is
provided is usual.

CHECKING OUT

Can I have an itemized bill/ a receipt?	**Kann ich eine aufgeschlüsselte Rechnung/Quittung haben?** *kahn eekh <u>ien</u> • uh owf • guh • <u>shlews</u> • ehlt • uh rekh • noong/ <u>kveet</u> • oong hah • buhn*
When's check-out?	**Wann ist der Check-out?** *vahn ihst dehr <u>tshehk</u> • owt*
Can I leave my bags here until…?	**Kann ich mein Gepäck bis … hierlassen?** *kahn eekh mien geh • <u>pehk</u> bihs … <u>heer</u> • lahs • uhn*
I think there's a mistake.	**Ich glaube, hier stimmt etwas nicht.** *eekh <u>glowb</u> • uh heer shtihmt <u>eht</u> • vahs neekht*
I'll pay in cash/by credit card.	**Ich bezahle bar/mit Kreditkarte.** *eekh beht • <u>sahl</u> • uh bahr/miht kreh • <u>deet</u> • kahrt • uh*

RENTING

I reserved an apartment/a room.	**Ich habe ein Apartment/ein Zimmer reserviert.** *eekh <u>hahb</u> • uh ien ah • <u>pahrt</u> • muhnt/ ien <u>tsihm</u> • mehr reh • sehr • <u>veert</u>*
My name is…	**Mein Name ist …** *mien <u>nahm</u> • uh ihst …*
Can I have the keys?	**Kann ich den Schlüssel haben?** *kahn eekh dehn <u>shlews</u> • suhl <u>hah</u> • buhn*
Are there…?	**Gibt es …?** *gihpt ehs …*
dishes	**Geschirr** *guh • <u>sheer</u>*

pillows	**Kissen**
	kihs • suhn
sheets	**Bettwäsche**
	beht • vehsh • uh
towels	**Handtücher**
	hahnt • tewkh • ehr
kitchen utensils	**Haushaltsgeräte**
	hows • hahlts • guh • reht • uh
When do I put out the bins/recycling?	**Wann stelle ich den Abfall/Müll raus?**
	vahn _shtehl_ • luh eekh dehn ahp • _fahl_/ mewl rows
...is broken.	**... funktioniert nicht.**
	... foonk • syoh • _neert_ neekht
How does...work?	**Wie funktioniert ...?**
	vee foonk • syoh • _neert_ ...
the air conditioner	**die Klimaanlage**
	dee _kleem_ • uh • ahn • lahg • uh
the dishwasher	**die Spülmaschine**
	dee _shpewl_ • mah • sheen • uh
the freezer	**der Gefrierschrank**
	dehr guh • _freer_ • shrahnk
the heating	**die Heizung**
	dee _hiet_ • soong
the microwave	**die Mikrowelle**
	dee mee • kroh • _vehl_ • luh
the refrigerator	**der Kühlschrank**
	dehr _kewhl_ • shrahnk
the stove	**der Herd**
	dehr hehrd
the washing machine	**die Waschmaschine**
	dee _vahsh_ • mah • shee • nuh

DOMESTIC ITEMS

I need...	**Ich brauche ...**
	eekh browkh • uh ...
an adapter	**einen Adapter**
	ien • uhn ah • dahp • tehr
aluminum [kitchen] foil	**Alufolie**
	ah • loo • foh • lee • uh
a bottle opener	**einen Flaschenöffner**
	ien • uhn flahsh • uhn • erf • nehr
a broom	**einen Besen**
	ien • uhn behz • uhn
a can opener	**einen Dosenöffner**
	ien • uhn doh • suhn • erf • nehr
cleaning supplies	**Reinigungsmittel**
	rien • ee • goongs • miht • tuhl
a corkscrew	**einen Korkenzieher**
	ien • uhn kohrk • uhn • tsee • ehr
detergent	**Waschmittel**
	vahsh • miht • tuhl
dishwashing liquid	**Geschirrspülmittel**
	guh • sheer • shpewl • miht • tuhl
bin bags	**Abfallsäcke**
	ahb • fahl • seh • khuh
a lightbulb	**eine Glühbirne**
	ien • uh glewh • beer • nuh
matches	**Streichhölzer**
	shtriekh • herlt • sehr
a mop	**einen Wischmopp**
	ien • uhn vihsh • mohp
napkins	**Servietten**
	sehr • vyeht • tuhn
paper towels	**Küchenrollen**
	kewkh • uhn • rohl • luhn

plastic wrap [cling film]	**Frischhaltefolie** _frihsh • hahl • tuh • foh • lee • uh_
a plunger	**eine Saugglocke** _ien • uh zowg • lohk • uh_
scissors	**eine Schere** _ien • uh shehr • uh_
a vacuum cleaner	**einen Staubsauger** _ien • uhn shtowb • sowg • ehr_

For In the Kitchen, see page 190.

AT THE HOSTEL

Is there a bed available?	**Haben Sie ein Bett frei?** _hah • buhn zee ien beht frie_
Can I have...?	**Kann ich ... haben?** _kahn eekh ... hah • buhn_
a single/double room	**ein Einzelzimmer/Doppelzimmer** _ien ient • sehl • tsihm • mehr/ dohp • pehl • tsihm • muhr_
a blanket	**eine Decke** _ien • uh dehk • huh_
a pillow	**ein Kissen** _icn kihs • suhn_
sheets	**Bettwäsche** _beht • vehsh • uh_
a towel	**ein Handtuch** _ien hahnt • tookh_
Do you have lockers?	**Haben Sie Schließfächer?** _hah • buhn zee shlees • fehkh • ehr_
When do you lock up?	**Wann schließen Sie ab?** _vahn shlees • suhn zee ahp_

ⓘ

There are more than 500 hostels throughout Germany, in cities large and small and in rural locations. You may need a Hostelling International membership card to stay at these hostels, many of which belong to **Deutsches Jugendherbergswerk (DJV)**. Hostels are inexpensive accommodations that offer dormitory-style rooms and, sometimes, private or semi-private rooms. Some offer private bathrooms, though most have shared facilities. There is usually a self-service kitchen on site. Booking in advance is a good idea, especially in large cities during festivals or holidays. Reservations can be made over the phone or online. Visit the Hostelling International website for more information.

Do I need a membership card?	**Brauche ich eine Mitgliedskarte?** _browkh • uh eekh ien • uh miht • gleeds • kahrt • uh_
Here's my international student card.	**Hier ist mein internationaler Studentenausweis.** _heer ihst mien ihn • tehr • nah • syoh • nahl • ehr shtoo • dehnt • uhn • ows • vies_

GOING CAMPING

Can I camp here?	**Kann ich hier campen?** _kahn eekh heer kahmp • uhn_
Where's the campsite?	**Wo ist der Campingplatz?** _voh ihst dehr kahmp • eeng • plahts_
What is the charge per day/week?	**Was kostet es pro Tag/Woche?** _vahs kohst • uht ehs proh tahk/vohkh • uh_

Are there...?	**Gibt es ...?**
	gihpt ehs ...
cooking facilities	**Kochmöglichkeiten**
	kohkh • merg • leekh • kiet • uhn
electric outlets	**Steckdosen**
	shtehkh • dohz • uhn
laundry facilities	**Waschmaschine**
	vahsh • maksch • een • uh
showers	**Duschen**
	doosh • uhn
tents for hire	**Mietzelte**
	meet • tsehl • tuh
Where can I empty the chemical toilet?	**Wo kann ich die Campingtoilette leeren?**
	voh kahn eekh dee kahmp • eeng • toy • leh • tuh lehr • uhn

For Domestic Items, see page 82.

YOU MAY SEE...

👁

TRINKWASSER	drinking water
ZELTEN VERBOTEN	no camping
OFFENES FEUER VERBOTEN	no fires

COMMUNICATIONS

NEED TO KNOW

Where's an internet cafe?	**Wo gibt es ein Internetcafé?** *voh gihpt ehs ien ihnt • ehr • neht • kah • feh*
Can I access the internet/check e-mail?	**Kann ich das Internet benutzen/ meine E-Mails lesen?** *kahn eekh dahs ihnt • ehr • neht beh • noot • suhn/mien • uh ee • miels lehz • uhn*
How much per (half) hour?	**Wie viel kostet eine (halbe) Stunde?** *vee feel kohst • uht ien • uh (hahlb • uh) shtoond • uh*
How do I log on?	**Wie melde ich mich an?** *vee mehld • uh eekh meekh ahn*
A phone card, please.	**Eine Telefonkarte, bitte.** *ien • uh tehl • uh • fohn • kahrt • uh biht • tuh*
Can I have your phone number?	**Kann ich Ihre Telefonnummer haben?** *kahn eekh eehr • uh tehl • uh • fohn • noom • ehr hah • buhn*
Here's my number/e-mail.	**Hier ist meine Telefonnummer/ E-Mail.** *heer ihst mien • uh tehl • uh • fohn • noom • ehr/ ee • miel*
Call me.	**Rufen Sie mich an.** *roo • fuhn zee meekh ahn*
E-mail me.	**Mailen Sie mir.** *miel • uhn zee meer*

Hello. This is…	**Hallo. Hier ist …**
	hah • loh heer ihst …
Can I speak to…?	**Kann ich mit … sprechen?**
	kahn eekh miht … shprehkh • uhn
Can you repeat that, please?	**Könnten Sie das bitte wiederholen?**
	kern • tuhn zee dahs biht • tuh veed • ehr • hohl • uhn
I'll call back later.	**Ich rufe später zurück.**
	eekh roof • uh shpeht • ehr tsoo • rewkh
Bye.	**Auf Wiederhören.**
	owf veed • ehr • her • ruhn
Where's the post office?	**Wo ist die Post?**
	voh ihst dee pohst
I'd like to send this to…	**Ich möchte das nach … schicken.**
	eekh merkh • tuh dahs nahkh … shihk • uhn

ONLINE

Where's an internet cafe?	**Wo gibt es ein Internetcafé?**
	voh gihpt ehs ien ihnt • ehr • neht • kah • feh
Does it have wireless internet?	**Gibt es dort wireless Internet?**
	gihpt ehs dohrt wier • luhs ihnt • ehr • neht
What is the WiFi password?	**Wie lautet das WLAN-Passwort?**
	vee low • teht dahs veh • lahn • pahs • vohrt
Is the WiFi free?	**Ist der WLAN-Zugang gratis?**
	ihst dehr veh • lahn • tsoo • gahng grah • tihs
Do you have bluetooth?	**Haben Sie Bluetooth?**
	hah • buhn zee bloo • tooth
How do I turn the computer on/off?	**Wie schalte ich den Computer an/aus?**
	vee shahlt • uh eekh dehn kohm • pjoot • ehr ahn/ows

Can I...?	**Kann ich ...?**
	kahn eekh ...
access the internet	**das Internet benutzen**
	dahs ihnt • ehr • neht beh • noot • suhn
check e-mail	**E-Mails lesen**
	ee • miels lehz • uhn
print	**drucken**
	drook • uhn
plug in/charge my laptop/iPhone/ iPad/BlackBerry?	**meinen Laptop/mein iPhone/iPad/ BlackBerry aufladen?**
	kahn eehk mien • uhn lap • top/mien iphone/ipad/blackberry owf • lahd • uhn
access Skype?	**Skype verwenden?**
	skype fuhr • vehn • dehn
use any computer	**einen Computer benutzen**
	ien • uhn kohm • pjoot • ehr beh • noot • suhn
How much per (half) hour?	**Wie viel kostet eine (halbe) Stunde?**
	vee feel kohst • uht ien • uh (hahlb • uh) shtoond • uh
How...?	**Wie ...?**
	vee ...
do I connect	**stelle ich eine Verbindung her**
	shteh • luh eekh ien • uh fuhr • bihnd • oong hehr
do I disconnect	**trenne ich eine Verbindung**
	trehn • uh eekh ien • uh fuhr • bihnd • oong
do I log on/off	**melde ich mich an/ab**
	mehld • uh eekh meekh ahn/ahp
do I type this symbol	**gebe ich dieses Zeichen ein**
	geh • buh eekh deez • uhs tsiekh • ehn ien
What's your e-mail?	**Wie ist Ihre E-Mail-Adresse?**
	vee ihst eehr • uh ee • miel • ah • drehs • uh
My e-mail is...	**Meine E-Mail-Adresse ist ...**
	mien • uh ee • miel • ah • drehs • uh ihst ...

Do you have a scanner?	**Haben Sie einen Scanner?**
	hah • buhn zee ien • uhn scan • nuhr

YOU MAY SEE... 👁

SCHLIESSEN	close
LÖSCHEN	delete
E-MAIL	e-mail
BEENDEN	exit
HILFE	help
INSTANT MESSENGER	instant messenger
INTERNET	internet
ANMELDEN	login
NEUE NACHRICHT	new message
AN/AUS	on/off
ÖFFNEN	open
DRUCKEN	print
SPEICHERN	save
SENDEN	send
BENUTZERNAME/PASSWORT	username/ password
WIRELESS INTERNET	wireless internet

SOCIAL MEDIA

Are you on Facebook/Twitter?	**Sind Sie bei Facebook/Twitter?** *(polite form)* *zihnt zee by face • book/twit • ter* **Bist du bei Facebook/Twitter?** *(informal form)* *bihst doo by face • book/twit • ter*
What's your user name?	**Was ist Ihr Benutzername?** *(polite form)* *vahs ihst eehr beh • noots • uhr • nah • muh* **Was ist dein Benutzername?** *(informal form)* *vahs ihst dien beh • noots • uhr • nah • muh*
I'll follow you on Twitter.	**Ich werde Ihre Twitter-Einträge verfolgen.** *(polite form)* *eekh vehr • duh eer • he twit • ter • ien • treh • ghe fehr • folg • hun* **Ich werde deine Twitter-Einträge verfolgen.** *(informal form)* *eekh vehr • duh die • nuh twit • ter • ien • treh • ghe fehr • folg • hun*
Are you following...?	**Verfolgen Sie ...?** *(polite form)* *fehr • folg • hun zee …* **Verfolgst du ...?** *(informal form)* *fehr • folgst doo …*
I'll add you as a friend.	**Ich werde Sie als Freund/Freundin hinzufügen.** *(polite form)* *eekh vehrd • uh zee ahls froynd/froyn • dihn hihn • tsoo • few • guhn* **Ich werde dich als Freund/Freundin hinzufügen.** *(informal form)* *eekh vehrd • uh deekh ahls froynd/froyn • dihn hihn • tsoo • few • guhn*

I'll put the pictures on Facebook/Twitter.
Ich werde die Fotos auf Facebook/ Twitter hochladen.
eekh vehr•duh dee foh•tohs owf face•book/ twit•ter hokh•lah•duhn

I'll tag you in the pictures.
Ich werde Sie auf den Fotos markieren.
(polite form)
eekh vehr•duh zee owf dehn foh•tohs mahr•kih•ruhn

Ich werde dich auf den Fotos markieren.
(informal form)
eekh vehr•duh deekh owf dehn foh•tohs mahr•kih•ruhn

YOU MAY SEE...

SCHLIESSEN	close
LÖSCHEN	delete
E-MAIL	e-mail
BEENDEN	exit
HILFE	help
INSTANT MESSENGER	instant messenger
INTERNET	internet
ANMELDEN	login
NEUE NACHRICHT	new message
AN/AUS	on/off
ÖFFNEN	open
DRUCKEN	print
SPEICHERN	save
SENDEN	send
BENUTZERNAME/PASSWORT	username/ password
WIRELESS INTERNET	wireless internet

PHONE

A phone card, please.	**Eine Telefonkarte, bitte.**
	ien • uh tehl • eh • fohn • kahrt • uh biht • tuh
A prepaid phone please.	**Ein Prepaid-Handy, bitte.**
	ien pree • paid han • dee biht • tuh
An international phonecard for…	**Eine internationale Telefonkarte für …**
	ien • uh ihnt • ehr • nah • syoh • nahl • uh tehl • uh • fohn • kahrt • uh fewr …
Australia	**Australien**
	ow • shtrah • lee • ehn
Canada	**Kanada**
	kah • nah • dah
Ireland	**Irland**
	eer • lahnt
the U.K.	**Großbritannien**
	grohs • bree • tahn • ee • ehn
the U.S.	**die USA**
	dee oo • ehs • ah
How much?	**Wie viel kostet es?**
	vee feel kohs • tuht ehs
Where's the pay phone?	**Wo ist das Münztelefon?**
	voh ihst dahs mewnts • tehl • uh • fohn
What's the area code/country code for…?	**Was ist die Ortsvorwahl/Landesvorwahl für …?**
	vahs ihst dee ohrts • fohr • vahl/ lahnd • uhs • fohr • vahl fewr …
What's the number for Information?	**Was ist die Nummer für die Auskunft?**
	vahs ihst dee noom • ehr fewr dee ows • kuhnft
I'd like the number for…	**Ich hätte gern die Nummer für …**
	eekh heht • uh gehrn dee noom • ehr fewr …

I'd like to call collect [reverse the charges]. **Ich möchte ein R-Gespräch führen.**
eekh merkh • tuh ien ehr • guh • shprehkh fewhr • uhn

My phone doesn't work here. **Mein Telefon funktioniert hier nicht.**
mien tehl • leh • fohn foonk • syoh • neert heer neekht

What network are you on? **Welches Netz nutzen Sie?**
vehl • khehs nehts noot • suhn zee

YOU MAY HEAR...

Ruff an?
roof ahn
Who's calling?

Einen Moment, bitte.
ien • uhn moh • mehnt biht • tuh
Hold on, please.

Ich verbinde Sie.
eekh fehr • bihnd • uh zee
I'll put you through.

Er m /Sie f ist nicht da/spricht gerade.
ehr/zee ihst neekht dah/shpreekht geh • rahd • uh
He/She is not here/on another line.

Möchten Sie eine Nachricht hinterlassen?
merkh • tuhn zee ien • uh nahkh • reekht hihnt • ehr • lahs • suhn
Would you like to leave a message?

Bitte rufen Sie später/in zehn Minuten zurück.
biht • tuh roof • uhn zee shpeht • ehr/ ihn tsehn mee • noot • uhn tsoo • rewkh
Please call back later/in ten minutes.

Kann er m /sie f zurückrufen?
khan ehr/zee tsoo • rewkh • roof • uhn
Can he/she call you back?

Was ist Ihre Nummer?
vahs ihst eehr • uh noom • ehr
What's your number?

Is it 3G?	**Ist es ein 3G-Netz?**
	ihst ehs ien drie • geh • nehts
I have run out of credit/minutes.	**Ich habe kein Guthaben mehr.**
	eekh hah • buh kien goot • hah • buhn mehr
Can I buy some credit?	**Kann ich eine Guthabenkarte kaufen?**
	kahn eekh ie • nuh
	goot • hah • buhn • kahr • tuh kow • fuhn
Do you have a phone charger?	**Haben Sie ein Handy-Ladegerät?**
	hah • buhn zee ien
	han • dee • lah • duh • guh • reht
Can I recharge this phone?	**Kann ich dieses Telefon wieder aufladen?**
	kahn eekh <u>deez</u> • uhs tehl • uh • <u>fohn</u> veed • ehr owf • <u>lahd</u> • uhn
Can I have your number, please?	**Können Sie mir bitte Ihre Nummer geben?**
	<u>kern</u> • uhn zee meer <u>biht</u> • tuh eehr • uh <u>noom</u> • ehr <u>gehb</u> • uhn

---

German public phones are mainly card operated.
Phone cards in various amounts can be purchased at
newsstands, supermarkets and other shops.
Important telephone numbers include:
Police 110
Fire 112
Ambulance 115
National Directory 11833
National Directory (in English) 11837
International Directory 11834
To call the U.S. or Canada from Germany, dial 001 + area
code + phone number. To call the U.K. from Germany, dial
0044 + area code (minus the first 0) + phone number.

Here's my number.	**Hier ist meine Nummer.**
	heer ihst mien • uh noom • ehr
Please call me.	**Bitte rufen Sie mich an.**
	biht • tuh roof • uhn zee meekh ahn
Please text me.	**Bitte schicken Sie mir eine SMS.**
	bit • tuh shihk • uhn zee meer ien • uh
	ehs • ehm • ehs
I'll call you.	**Ich werde Sie anrufen.**
	eekh vehrd • uh zee ahn • roof • uhn
I'll text you.	**Ich werde Ihnen eine SMS schicken.**
	eekh vehrd • uh eehn • uhn ien • uh
	ehs • ehm • ehs shihk • uhn

TELEPHONE ETIQUETTE

Hello. This is…	**Hallo. Hier ist …**
	hahl • loh heer ihst …
Can I speak to…?	**Kann ich mit … sprechen?**
	kahn eekh miht … shprehkh • uhn
Extension…	**Durchwahl …**
	doorkh • vahl …
Speak louder/more slowly, please.	**Bitte sprechen Sie lauter/langsamer.**
	biht • tuh shprehkh • uhn zee lowt • ehr/ lahng • sahm • ehr
Can you repeat that, please?	**Könnten Sie das bitte wiederholen?**
	kern • tuhn zee dahs biht • tuh vee • dehr • hohl • uhn
I'll call back later.	**Ich rufe später zurück.**
	eekh roof • uh shpeht • ehr tsoo • rewkh
Bye.	**Auf Wiederhören.**
	owf veed • ehr • her • ruhn

For Communications, see page 86.

FAX

Can I send/receive a fax here?	**Kann ich hier ein Fax senden/ empfangen?**
	kahn eekh heer ien fahks <u>zehnd</u> • uhn/ <u>ehm</u> • pfahng • uhn
What's the fax number?	**Was ist die Faxnummer?**
	vahs ihst dee <u>fahks</u> • noom • ehr
Please fax this to…	**Bitte faxen Sie das nach …**
	<u>biht</u> • tuh <u>fahks</u> • uhn zee dahs nahkh …

POST

Where's the post office/mailbox?	**Wo ist die Post/der Briefkasten?**
	voh ihst dee pohst/dehr <u>breef</u> • kahs • tuhn
A stamp for this postcard/letter to…, please.	**Eine Briefmarke für diese Postkarte/ diesen Brief nach … bitte.**
	<u>ien</u> • uh <u>breef</u> • mahrk • uh fewr <u>deez</u> • uh <u>pohst</u> • kahrt • uh/<u>deez</u> • uhn breef nahkh … biht • tuh
How much?	**Wie viel kostet das?**
	vee feel <u>kohs</u> • tuht dahs

YOU MAY HEAR...

Bitte füllen Sie das Zollformular aus.
biht • tuh fewl • luhn zee dahs
tsohl • fohr • moo • lahr ows

Fill out the customs declaration form, please.

Wie viel ist es wert?
vee feel ihst ehs vehrt

What's the value?

Was ist der Inhalt?
vahs ihst dehr ihn • hahlt

What's inside?

Please send this package by airmail/express.

Senden Sie dieses Paket bitte per Luftpost/Express.
zehnd • uhn zee deez • uhs pah • keht
biht • tuh pehr looft • pohst/ehks • prehs

A receipt, please.

Eine Quittung, bitte.
ien • uh kveet • toong biht • tu

In addition to mailing options, German post offices offer a variety of other services. Most provide banking services and allow you to deposit or withdraw money and apply for a credit card. On weekdays, post offices are usually open from 8:30 a.m. to 1:00 p.m., and again from 2:30 p.m. to 4:00 p.m. (in larger cities to 6:30 p.m.). On Saturdays they are open from 8:30 a.m. to 1:00 p.m.

NEED TO KNOW

Where's the tourist information office?	**Wo ist das Touristeninformationsbüro?** *voh ihst dahs* *too • <u>ree</u> • stuhn • een • fohr • mah • syohns • bew • roh*
What are the main sights?	**Was sind die wichtigsten Sehenswürdigkeiten?** *vahs zihnt dee <u>veekh</u> • teeg • stuhn* *<u>zeh</u> • uhns • vewr • deekh • kie • tuhn*
Do you offer tours in English?	**Haben Sie Führungen in Englisch?** *<u>hah</u> • buhn zee <u>few</u> • roong • uhn een* *ehn • gleesh*
Can I have a map/ guide?	**Kann ich einen Stadtplan/ Reiseführer haben?** *kahn eekh <u>ien</u> • uhn <u>shtaht</u> • plahn/* *rie • seh • <u>fewhr</u> • ehr <u>hah</u> • buhn*

TOURIST INFORMATION

Do you have information on...?
Haben Sie Informationen über ...?
hah • buhn zee
ihn • fohr • mah • syoh • nuhn ew • buhr ...

Can you recommend...?
Können Sie ... empfehlen?
ker • nuhn zee ... ehm • pfeh • luhn

a bus tour
eine Busreise
ien • uh boos • rie • zuh

an excursion to...
einen Ausflug nach ...
ien • uhn ows • flook nahkh ...

a sightseeing tour
eine Stadtrundfahrt
ien • uh shtaht • roond • fahrt

ON TOUR

I'd like to go on the tour to...
Ich möchte gern an der ... Führung teilnehmen.
eekh merkht • uh gehrn ahn dehr ...
fewhr • oong tiel • nehm • uhn

When's the next tour?
Wann ist die nächste Führung?
vahn ihst dee nehkhst • uh fewhr • oong

Are there tours in English?
Gibt es Führungen in Englisch?
gihpt ehs fewhr • oong • uhn ihn
ehng • lihsh

Is there an English guide book/audio guide?
Gibt es einen englischsprachigen Reiseführer/Audio-Guide?
gihpt ehs ien • uhn
ehng • lihsh • shprahkh • ee • guhn
riez • uh • fewhr • ehr/ow • dee • oh • gied

What time do we leave/return?
Wann fahren wir ab/kommen wir wieder?
vahn fahhr • uhn veer ap/kohm • uhn veer
veed • ehr

We'd like to see…	**Wir möchten gern … sehen.**
	veer merkht • uhn gehrn … zeh • uhn
Can we stop here…?	**Können wir hier anhalten …?**
	ker • nuhn veer heer ahn • hahlt • uhn …
to take photos	**um Fotos zu machen**
	oom foht • ohs tsoo mahkh • uhn
for souvenirs	**um Andenken zu kaufen**
	oom ahn • dehnk • uhn tsoo kowf • uhn
for the toilets	**um auf die Toilette zu gehen**
	oom owf dee toy • leht • uh tsoo geh • uhn
Is it disabled-accessible?	**Ist es behindertengerecht?**
	ihst ehs beh • hihn • dehrt • uhn • geh • rehkht

For Tickets, see page 47.

SEEING THE SIGHTS

Where's…?	**Wo ist …?**
	voh ihst …
the battleground	**das Schlachtfeld**
	dahs shlahkht • fehlt
the botanical garden	**der botanische Garten**
	dehr boh • tahn • eesh • uh gahr • tuhn
the castle	**das Schloss**
	dahs shlohs
the downtown area	**das Stadtzentrum**
	dahs shtadt • tsehnt • room
the fountain	**der Brunnen**
	dehr broon • uhn
the library	**die Bücherei**
	dee bewkh • eh • rie
the market	**der Markt**
	dehr mahrkt
the museum	**das Museum**
	dahs moo • zeh • oom

ⓘ

Tourist information offices are located throughout
Germany. Look for the 'i' symbol or ask your hotel concierge
where the nearest office is located. Tourist information
offices can recommend destinations, attractions, local
events and festivals, and help you find hotels, tours,
transportation and other services. Visit the **Deutsche
Zentrale für Tourismus**, **DZT** (German center for tourism),
website for more information.

the old town	**die Altstadt**	
	dee _ahlt_ • shtahdt	
the opera house	**das Opernhaus**	
	dahs _oh_ • pehrn • hows	
the palace	**der Palast**	
	dehr pah • _lahst_	
the park	**der Park**	
	dehr pahrk	
the ruins	**die Ruine**	
	dee ro • _ee_ • nuh	
the shopping area	**das Einkaufszentrum**	
	dahs _ien_ • kowfs • tsehn • troom	
the theater	**das Theater**	
	dahs teh • _ah_ • tehr	
the tower	**der Turm**	
	dehr toorm	
the town hall	**das Rathaus**	
	dahs _raht_ • hows	
the town square	**der Rathausplatz**	
	dehr _raht_ • hows • plats	

Can you show me on the map?	**Können Sie mir das im Stadtplan zeigen?**
	ker • _nuhn zee meer dahs ihm_ _shtadt_ • _plahn tsie_ • _guhn_
It's…	**Es ist …**
	ehs ihst …
amazing	**erstaunlich**
	ehr • _shtown_ • _leekh_
beautiful	**wunderschön**
	voond • _ehr_ • _shern_
boring	**langweilig**
	lahng • _viel_ • _eek_
interesting	**interessant**
	ihn • _teh_ • _reh_ • _sahnt_
magnificent	**großartig**
	groh • _sahr_ • _teek_
romantic	**romantisch**
	roh • _mahnt_ • _eesh_
strange	**seltsam**
	zehlt • _zahm_
stunning	**umwerfend**
	oom • _vehrf_ • _uhnt_
terrible	**schrecklich**
	shrehk • _leekh_
ugly	**hässlich**
	hehs • _leekh_
I (don't) like it.	**Es gefällt mir (nicht).**
	ehs guh • _fehlt meer (neekht)_

For Grammar, see page 12.

RELIGIOUS SITES

Where's…?	**Wo ist …?** *voh ihst …*
the cathedral	**die Kathedrale** *dee kah • teh • <u>drahl</u> • uh*
the Catholic/ Protestant church	**die katholische/evangelische Kirche** *dee kah • <u>toh</u> • leesh • uh/ eh • vahn • <u>gehl</u> • eesh • uh <u>keer</u> • khuh*
the mosque	**die Moschee** *dee moh • <u>sheh</u>*
the shrine	**der Schrein** *dehr shrien*
the synagogue	**die Synagoge** *dee zewn • uh • <u>goh</u> • guh*
the temple	**der Tempel** *dehr <u>tehm</u> • pehl*
What time is mass/ the service?	**Wann ist die Messe/der Gottesdienst?** *vahn ihst dee <u>mehs</u> • suh/dehr <u>goht</u> • ehs • deenst*

ACTIVITIES

SHOPPING

NEED TO KNOW

Where's the market/ mall [shopping centre]?	**Wo ist der Markt/das Einkaufszentrum?** *voh ihst dehr mahrkt/dahs <u>ien</u> • kowfs • tsehn • troom*
I'm just looking.	**Ich schaue mich nur um.** *eekh <u>show</u> • uh meekh noor oom*
Can you help me?	**Können Sie mir helfen?** *<u>kern</u> • uhn zee meer <u>hehlf</u> • uhn*
I'm being helped.	**Ich werde schon bedient.** *eekh <u>vehrd</u> • uh shohn beh • <u>deent</u>*
How much?	**Wie viel kostet das?** *vee feel <u>kohs</u> • tuht dahs*
That one, please.	**Dieses bitte.** *<u>dee</u> • zuhs <u>biht</u> • tuh*
That's all.	**Das ist alles.** *dahs ihst <u>ahl</u> • uhs*
Where can I pay?	**Wo kann ich bezahlen?** *voh kahn eekh beh • <u>tsahl</u> • uhn*
I'll pay in cash/by credit card.	**Ich zahle bar/mit Kreditkarte.** *eekh tsahl • uh bahr/miht kreh • <u>deet</u> • kahr • tuh*
A receipt, please.	**Eine Quittung, bitte.** *<u>ien</u> • uh <u>kvih</u> • toong <u>biht</u> • tuh*

AT THE SHOPS

Where's...?	**Wo ist ...?** *voh ihst ...*

the antiques store	**das Antiquitätengeschäft** *dahs ahn • tee • kwee • tay • tuhn • guh • shehft*
the bakery	**die Bäckerei** *dee beh • keh • rie*
the bank	**die Bank** *dee bahnk*
the bookstore	**der Buchladen** *dehr bookh • lahd • uhn*
the clothing store	**das Bekleidungsgeschäft** *dahs buh • klied • oongs • guh • shehft*
the delicatessen	**das Feinkostgeschäft** *dahs fien • kohst • guh • shehft*
the department store	**das Kaufhaus** *dahs kowf • hows*
the gift shop	**der Geschenkwarenladen** *dehr guh • shehnk • vah • ruhn • lah • duhn*
the health food store	**das Reformhaus** *dahs reh • fohrm • hows*
the jeweler	**das Schmuckgeschäft** *dahs shmook • guh • shehft*
the liquor store [off-licence]	**das Spirituosengeschäft** *dahs shpee • ree • twoh • zuhn • guh • shehft*
the market	**der Markt** *dehr mahrkt*
the music store	**das Musikgeschäft** *dahs moo • zeek • guh • shehft*
the pastry shop	**die Konditorei** *dee kohn • dee • toh • rie*
the pharmacy [chemist]	**die Apotheke** *dee ah • poh • tehk • uh*
the produce [grocery] store	**das Lebensmittelgeschäft** *dahs lehb • uhns • miht • uhl • guh • shehft*
the shoe store	**das Schuhgeschäft** *dahs shooh • guh • shehft*

the shopping mall [shopping centre]	**das Einkaufszentrum** *dahs <u>ien</u> • kowfs • tsehn • troom*
the souvenir store	**der Andenkenladen** *dehr <u>ahn</u> • dehnk • uhn • lah • duhn*
the supermarket	**der Supermarkt** *dehr <u>zoo</u> • pehr • mahrkt*
the tobacconist	**der Tabakladen** *dehr tah • <u>bahk</u> • lahd • uhn*
the toy store	**das Spielzeuggeschäft** *<u>peel</u> • tsoyg • geh • shehft*

ASK AN ASSISTANT

When do you open/close?	**Wann öffnen/schließen Sie?** *vahn <u>erf</u> • nuhn/<u>shlees</u> • uhn zee*
Where's…?	**Wo ist …?** *voh ihst …*
the cashier	**die Kasse** *dee <u>kah</u> • suh*
the escalator	**die Rolltreppe** *dee <u>rohl</u> • trehp • uh*
the elevator [lift]	**der Fahrstuhl** *dehr <u>fahr</u> • shtool*
the fitting room	**die Umkleidekabine** *dee <u>oom</u> • klied • uh • kah • bee • nuh*
the store directory	**die Liste mit den Geschäften?** *dee lihs • tuh miht dehn guh • sheft • tuhn*
Can you help me?	**Können Sie mir helfen?** *<u>kern</u> • uhn zee meer <u>hehl</u> • fuhn*
I'm just looking.	**Ich schaue mich nur um.** *eekh <u>show</u> • uh meekh noor oom*
I'm already being helped.	**Ich werde schon bedient.** *eekh <u>vehrd</u> • uh shohn buh • <u>deent</u>*
Do you have…?	**Haben Sie …?** *<u>hah</u> • buhn zee …*

YOU MAY HEAR...

Kann ich Ihnen helfen?
kahn eekh <u>eehn</u> • uhn <u>hehlf</u> • uhn
Can I help you?

Einen Moment.
<u>ien</u> • uhn moh • <u>mehnt</u>
One moment.

Was möchten Sie?
vahs <u>merkht</u> • uhn zee
What would you like?

Noch etwas?
nohkh <u>eht</u> • vahs
Anything else?

Can you show me...?	**Können Sie mir ... zeigen?** *<u>kern</u> • nuhn zee meer ... <u>tsieg</u> • uhn*
Can you ship/wrap it?	**Können Sie das versenden/einpacken?** *<u>kern</u> • uhn zee dahs fehr • <u>zehn</u> • duhn/ <u>ien</u> • pahk • uhn*
How much?	**Wie viel kostet es?** *vee feel <u>kohs</u> • tuht ehs*
That's all.	**Das ist alles.** *dahs ihst <u>ahl</u> • uhs*

For Clothing, see page 117.

PERSONAL PREFERENCES

I'd like something...	**Ich möchte etwas ...** *eekh <u>merkht</u> • uh <u>eht</u> • vahs ...*
cheap/expensive	**Billiges/Teueres** *<u>bihl</u> • ee • guhs/<u>toy</u> • ehr • uhs*
larger/smaller	**Größeres/Kleineres** *<u>grers</u> • eh • ruhs/<u>klien</u> • eh • ruhs*
nicer	**Schöneres** *<u>shern</u> • uh • ruhs*

YOU MAY SEE...

GEÖFFNET/GESCHLOSSEN	open/closed
ÜBER MITTAG GESCHLOSSEN	closed for lunch
EINGANG	entrance
UMKLEIDEKABINE	fitting room
KASSE	cashier
NUR BARZAHLUNG MÖGLICH	cash only
KREDITKARTENZAHLUNG MÖGLICH	credit cards accepted
ÖFFNUNGSZEITEN	business hours
AUSGANG	exit

from this region	**aus dieser Region**
	ows deez • ehr rehg • yohn
Around...euros.	**Ungefähr ... Euro.**
	oon • guh • fehr ... oy • roh
Can you show me...?	**Können Sie mir ... zeigen?**
	kern • uhn zee meer ... tsieg • uhn
Is it real?	**Ist das echt?**
	ihst dahs ehkht
That's not quite what I want.	**Das ist nicht ganz das, was ich möchte.**
	dahs ihst neekht gahnts dahs vahs eekh merkht • uh
No, I don't like it.	**Das gefällt mir nicht.**
	dahs guh • fehlt meer neekht
It's too expensive.	**Es ist zu teuer.**
	ehs ihst tsoo toy • ehr
I have to think about it.	**Das muss ich mir überlegen.**
	dahs moos eekh meer ewb • ehr • leh • guhn
I'll take it.	**Ich nehme es.**
	eekh nehm • uh ehs

PAYING & BARGAINING

How much?	**Wie viel kostet es?**
	vee feel <u>kohs</u> • tuht ehs
I'll pay...	**Ich zahle ...**
	eekh <u>tsah</u> • luh ...
in cash	**bar**
	bahr
by credit card	**mit Kreditkarte**
	miht kreh • <u>deet</u> • kahr • tuh
by traveler's cheque	**mit Reiseschecks**
	miht <u>riez</u> • uh • shehks
A receipt, please.	**Die Quittung, bitte.**
	dee <u>kviht</u> • oong biht • tuh
That's too much.	**Das ist zu viel.**
	dahs ihst tsoo veel
I'll give you...	**Ich gebe Ihnen ...**
	eekh <u>gehb</u> • uh eehn • uhn ...
I have only... euros.	**Ich habe nur ... Euro.**
	eekh <u>hah</u> • buh noor ... <u>oy</u> • roh

(i)

In Germany, cash is the preferred form of payment. Credit cards are accepted in most larger stores, gas stations, hotels and restaurants. Credit cards may not be accepted by smaller businesses, so be sure to ask before making a purchase. Traveler's checks are not very popular in Germany. If taken, they should be exchanged for cash at a currency exchange office or bank, though a fee will be charged for the exchange. Some banks do not accept traveler's checks.

Is that your best price?	**Ist das Ihr bester Preis?**
	ihst dahs eehr <u>behst</u> • ehr pries

| Can you give me a discount? | **Können Sie mir einen Rabatt geben?** |
| | _kern • uhn zee meer ien • uhn rah • baht geh • buhn_ |

For Numbers, see page 22.

MAKING A COMPLAINT

I'd like...	**Ich möchte ...**
	eekh merkht • uh ...
to exchange this	**das umtauschen**
	dahs oom • tow • shuhn
a refund	**gern mein Geld zurück**
	gehrn mien gehld tsoo • rewk
to see the manager	**mit dem Manager sprechen**
	miht dehm mahn • ah • jehr shprehkh • uhn

SERVICES

| Can you recommend...? | **Können Sie ... empfehlen?** |
| | _kern • uhn zee ... ehm • pfeh • luhn_ |

YOU MAY HEAR...

Wie möchten Sie zahlen?
vee merkht • uhn zee tsahl • uhn
How are you paying?

Ihre Kreditkarte wurde abgelehnt.
eehr • uh kreh • deet • kahr • tuh voor • duh ahp • guh • lehnt
Your credit card has been declined.

Ihren Ausweis, bitte.
eehr • uhn ows • vies biht • tuh
ID, please.

Wir nehmen keine Kreditkarten.
veer neh • muhn kie • nuh kreh • deet • kahr • tuhn
We don't accept credit cards.

Bitte nur Bargeld.
biht • tuh noor bahr • gehlt
Cash only, please.

Haben Sie Wechselgeld/kleine Scheine?
hah • buhn zee vehkh • zuhl • gehlt/ klien • uh shien • uh
Do you have change/small bills [notes]?

a barber	**einen Herrenfriseur**	
	ien • uhn hehr • uhn • frih • zer	
a dry cleaner	**eine Reinigung**	
	ien • uh rien • ee • goong	
a hairstylist	**einen Friseur**	
	ien • uhn frih • zer	
a laundromat [launderette]	**einen Waschsalon**	
	ien • uhn vahsh • zah • lohn	
a nail salon	**ein Nagelstudio**	
	ien nah • gehl • shtood • yoh	
a spa	**ein Wellness-Center**	
	ien vehl • nuhs • sehn • tehr	
a travel agency	**ein Reisebüro**	
	ien rie • zuh • bew • roh	

Can you...this?	**Können Sie das ...?**
	kern • uhn zee dahs ...
alter	**ändern**
	ehn • dehrn
clean	**reinigen**
	rien • ee • guhn
fix	**reparieren**
	reh • pah • _reer_ • uhn
press	**bügeln**
	bewg • uhln
When will it be ready?	**Wann wird es fertig sein?**
	vahn veerd ehs _fehr_ • teekh zien

HAIR & BEAUTY

I'd like...	**Ich möchte ...**
	eekh _merkht_ • uh ...
an appointment for today/tomorrow	**einen Termin für heute/morgen**
	ien • uhn tehr • _meen_ fewr _hoy_ • tuh/ _mohr_ • guhn
some color/ highlights	**die Haare/Strähnchen gefärbt bekommen**
	dee _hah_ • ruh/_shtrehnk_ • uhn guh • _ferbt_ buh • _kohm_ • uhn
my hair styled/ blow-dried	**mein Haar stylen/fönen lassen**
	mien hahr _shtew_ • luhn/_fern_ • uhn _lahs_ • uhn
a haircut	**einen Haarschnitt**
	ien • uhn hahr • shniht
an eyebrow/bikini wax	**eine Haarentfernung an den Augenbrauen/der Bikinizone**
	ien • uh hahr • ehnt • fehr • noong ahn dehn _ow_ • guhn • brow • uhn/dehr bee • _kee_ • nee • tsoh • nuh
a facial	**eine Gesichtsbehandlung**
	ien • uh guh • _zeekhts_ • beh • hahnd • loong

a manicure/ pedicure	**eine Maniküre/Pediküre** _ien_ • uh mahn • eh • kewruh/ pede • eh • kewruh
a (sports) massage	**eine (Sport-)Massage** _ien_ • uh (shport-) mah • _sahdj_ • uh
a trim	**die Haare nachschneiden lassen** dee _hahr_ • uh _nahkh_ • shnayd • uhn _lahs_ • uhn
Not too short.	**Nicht zu kurz.** neekht tsoo koorts
Shorter here.	**Hier kürzer.** heer _kewrts_ • ehr
Do you offer…?	**Machen Sie …?** mahk • uhn zee …
acupuncture	**Akupunktur** ah • koo • poonk • _toor_
aromatherapy	**Aromatherapie** ah • roh • mah • teh • _rah_ • pee
oxygen treatment	**Sauerstoffbehandlung** _zow_ • ehr • shtohf • beh • hahnd • loong
Do you have a sauna?	**Haben Sie eine Sauna?** _hah_ • buhn zee _ien_ • uh _zown_ • ah

(i)

Health resorts, day spas and hotel spas are popular destinations, and there are hundreds throughout Germany. Most spa towns have the word **Bad** in their names, for example: Bad Reichenhall, Europe's largest saline source, in Bavaria; Baden-Baden, considered the best and most fashionable; Wiesbaden, one of Germany's oldest cities and considered second best only to Baden-Baden; Bad Homburg, at the foot of Taunus Hills, once the summer retreat of Prussian kings; and Bad Nauheim, famous because both William Randolph Hearst and Elvis Presley were once guests experiencing the healing powers of the carbonic acid springs. Tipping varies by spa; ask about the tipping policy when booking or upon arrival.

ANTIQUES

How old is it?	**Wie alt ist es?** *vee ahlt ihst ehs*
Do you have anything from the… period?	**Haben Sie etwas aus der … Zeit?** *hah • buhn zee eht • vahs ows dehr … tsiet*
Do I have to fill out any forms?	**Muss ich irgendwelche Formulare ausfüllen?** *moos eekh eer • guhnd • vehlkh • uh fohr • moo • lahr • uh ows • fewl • uhn*
Is there a certificate of authenticity?	**Gibt es ein Echtheitszeugnis?** *gihpt ehs ien ehkht • hiets • tsoyg • nuhs*
Can you ship/ wrap it?	**Können Sie es liefern/einpacken?** *ker • nuhn zee ehs lee • fuhrn/ ien • pahk • kuhn*

CLOTHING

I'd like…	**Ich möchte …**
	eekh <u>merkht</u> • uh …
Can I try this on?	**Kann ich das anprobieren?**
	kahn eekh dahs <u>ahn</u> • proh • bee • ruhn
It doesn't fit.	**Es passt nicht.**
	ehs pahst neekht
It's too…	**Es ist zu …**
	ehs ihst tsoo …
big/small	**groß/klein**
	grohs/klien
short/long	**kurz/lang**
	koorts/lahng
tight/loose	**eng/weit**
	ehng/viet
Do you have this in size…?	**Haben Sie das in der Größe … ?**
	<u>hah</u> • buhn zee dahs ihn dehr <u>grers</u> • uh …
Do you have this in a bigger/smaller size?	**Haben Sie das in einer größeren/kleineren Größe?**
	<u>hah</u> • buhn zee dahs ihn <u>ien</u> • ehr <u>grers</u> • ehr • uhn/klien • uh • ruhn <u>grers</u> • uh

For Numbers, see page 22.

YOU MAY SEE…

HERRENABTEILUNG	men's (department)
DAMENABTEILUNG	women's (department)
KINDERABTEILUNG	children's (department)

COLORS

I'd like something…	**Ich möchte etwas …**
	eekh merkht • uh eht • vahs …
beige	**Beiges**
	behdj • uhs
black	**Schwarzes**
	shvahrtz • uhs
blue	**Blaues**
	blow • uhs
brown	**Braunes**
	brown • uhs
green	**Grünes**
	grewn • uhs
gray	**Graues**
	grow • uhs
orange	**Oranges**
	oh • rahnj • uhs
pink	**Pinkes**
	peenk • uhs
purple	**Violettes**
	vee • oh • leht • uhs
red	**Rotes**
	roht • uhs
white	**Weißes**
	vies • uhs
yellow	**Gelbes**
	gehlb • uhs

CLOTHES & ACCESSORIES

a backpack	**der Rucksack**
	dehr rook • zahk

a belt	**der Gürtel**
	dehr <u>gewrt</u> • uhl
a bikini	**der Bikini**
	dehr bih • <u>kee</u> • nee
a blouse	**die Bluse**
	dee <u>bloo</u> • zuh
a bra	**der BH**
	dehr beh • <u>hah</u>
briefs [underpants]	**der Schlüpfer**
	dehr <u>shlewp</u> • fehr
panties	**die Unterhosen**
	dee oont • ehr • hoh • suhn
a coat	**der Mantel**
	dehr <u>mahnt</u> • ehl
a dress	**das Kleid**
	dahs klied
a hat	**der Hut**
	dehr hoot
a jacket	**die Jacke**
	dee <u>yah</u> • kuh
jeans	**die Jeans**
	dee djeens
pajamas	**der Schlafanzug**
	dehr <u>shlahf</u> • ahn • tsoog
pants [trousers]	**die Hose**
	dee <u>hohz</u> • uh
pantyhose [tights]	**die Strumpfhose**
	dee <u>shtroompf</u> • hoh • zuh
a purse [handbag]	**die Handtasche**
	dee <u>hahnd</u> • tahsh • uh
a raincoat	**der Regenmantel**
	dehr <u>rehg</u> • uhn • mahn • tuhl
a scarf	**der Schal**
	dehr shahl

a shirt	**das Hemd**
	dahs hehmt
shorts	**die kurze Hose**
	dee koortz • uh hohz • uh
a skirt	**der Rock**
	dehr rohk
socks	**die Socken**
	dee zohk • uhn
a suit	**der Anzug**
	dehr ahn • tsoog
sunglasses	**die Sonnenbrille**
	dee zohn • uhn • brihl • uh
a sweater	**der Pullover**
	dehr pool • oh • fehr
a sweatshirt	**das Sweatshirt**
	dahs sveht • shehrt
a swimsuit	**der Badeanzug**
	dehr bah • deh • ahn • tsoog
a T-shirt	**das T-Shirt**
	dahs tee • shert
a tie	**die Krawatte**
	dee krah • vah • tuh
underwear	**die Unterwäsche**
	dee oon • tehr • vehsh • uh

YOU MAY HEAR...

Das steht Ihnen gut.	That looks great
dahs shteht eehn • uhn goot	on you.
Passt es?	How does it fit?
pahst ehs	
Wir führen Ihre Größe nicht.	We don't have
veer fewhr • uhn eehr • uh grers • uh neekht	your size.

FABRIC

I'd like…	**Ich möchte …**
	eekh merkht • uh …
cotton	**Baumwolle**
	bowm • vohl • uh
denim	**Denim**
	dehn • ihm
lace	**Spitze**
	shpihts • uh
leather	**Leder**
	lehd • ehr
linen	**Leinen**
	lien • uhn
silk	**Seide**
	zied • uh
wool	**Wolle**
	vohl • uh
Is it machine washable?	**Ist es waschmaschinenfest?**
	ihst ehs vahsh • mah • sheen • uhn • fehst

SHOES

I'd like...	**Ich möchte ...**
	eekh merkht • uh ...
high-heels/flats	**Schuhe mit Absatz/ohne Absatz**
	shoo • uh miht ahp • zahts/ohn • uh
	ahb • zahts
boots	**Stiefel**
	shtee • fuhl
loafers	**Slipper**
	slihp • ehr
sandals	**Sandalen**
	zahn • dahl • uhn
shoes	**Schuhe**
	shoo • uh
slippers	**Badelatschen**
	bah • duh • lahtsh • uhn
sneakers	**Turnschuhe**
	toorn • shoo • huh
In size...	**In der Größe ...**
	ihn dehr grers • uh ...

For Numbers, see page 22.

SIZES

small (S)	**klein**
	klein
medium (M)	**mittel**
	miht • tuhl
large (L)	**gross**
	grohs
extra large (XL)	**extra gross**
	ehks • trah grohs

petite	**die Kurzgröße**
	dee koorts • grer • suh
plus size	**die Übergröße**
	dee ew • buhr • grer • suh

(i)

In addition to small, medium and large, many clothing articles are labeled by continental size. As that size varies by manufacturer, be sure to try on any article before buying.

NEWSSTAND & TOBACCONIST

Do you sell English-language newspapers?	**Haben Sie englischsprachige Zeitungen?**
	hah • buhn zee
	ehng • leesh • shprah • khee • guh
	tsie • toong • uhn
I'd like...	**Ich möchte …**
	eekh merkht • uh …
candy [sweets]	**Süßigkeiten**
	zews • eekh • kiet • uhn
chewing gum	**Kaugummi**
	kow • goo • mee
a chocolate bar	**einen Schokoladenriegel**
	ien • uhn shoh • koh • lahd • uhn • ree • guhl
a cigar	**eine Zigarre**
	ien • uh tsee • gahr • uh
a pack/carton of	**eine Schachtel/Stange Zigaretten**
	ien • uh
cigarettes	*shahkht • uhl/shtahng • uh*
	tsee • gahr • eht • uhn
a lighter	**ein Feuerzeug**
	ien foy • ehr • tsoyg
a magazine	**eine Zeitschrift**
	ien • uh tsiet • shrihft

matches	**Streichhölzer**
	shtriekh • herlts • uhr
a newspaper	**eine Zeitung**
	ien • uh tsie • toong
a pen	**einen Stift**
	ien • uhn shtihft
a postcard	**eine Postkarte**
	ien • uh pohst • kahr • tuh
a road/town map of...	**eine Straßenkarte/einen Stadtplan vonen ...**
	ien • uh shtrahsuhn • kahrt • uh/ien • uhn shtaht • plahn fohn
stamps	**Briefmarken**
	breef • mahrk • uhn

PHOTOGRAPHY

I'd like a/an... camera.	**Ich möchte eine ... Kamera.**
	eekh merkht • uh ien • uh ... kah • meh • ruh
automatic	**automatische**
	ow • toh • maht • ihsh • uh
digital	**digitale**
	dihd • juh • tuhl
disposable	**Wegwerf-**
	vehk • vehrf-
I'd like...	**Ich möchte ...**
	eekh merkht • uh ...
a battery	**eine Batterie**
	ien • uh bah • tuh • ree
digital prints	**digitale Ausdrucke**
	dihd • juh • tuhl ows • drook • uh
a memory card	**eine Speicherkarte**
	ien • uh shpie • khuhr • kahrt • uh

Can I print digital photos here?	**Kann ich hier Digitalfotos ausdrucken lassen?**
	kahn eekh heer dih • jih • tahl • foh • tohs ows • droo • kuhn lahs • uhn

SOUVENIRS

Can I see this/that?	**Kann ich das sehen?**
	kahn eekh dahs zeh • uhn
It's in the window/ display case.	**Es ist im Schaufenster/In der Vitrine.**
	ehs ihst ihm schow • fehn • stehr/ihn dehr vih • tree • nuh
I'd like…	**Ich möchte …**
	eekh merkht • uh …
a battery	**eine Batterie**
	ien • uh bah • tuh • ree
a bracelet	**ein Armband**
	ien ahrm • bahnt
a brooch	**eine Brosche**
	ien • uh brohsh • uh
a clock	**eine Uhr**
	ien • uh oohr
earrings	**Ohrringe**
	oh • reeng • uh
a necklace	**eine Kette**
	ien • uh keht • uh
a ring	**einen Ring**
	ien • uhn reeng
a watch	**eine Uhr**
	ien • uh oohr
I'd like…	**Ich möchte …**
	eekh merkht • uh …
a beer stein	**einen Bierkrug**
	ien • uh beer • kroog

a bottle of wine	**eine Flasche Wein**
	ien • uh flahsh • uh vien
a box of	**eine Schachtel Pralinen**
chocolates	*ien • uh shahkht • uhl prah • lee • nuhn*
a doll	**eine Puppe**
	ien • uh poo • puh
a key ring	**ein Schlüsselring**
	ien shlews • uhl • reeng
a postcard	**eine Postkarte**
	ien • uh post • kahr • tuh
pottery	**Töpferwaren**
	terp • fuhr • vah • ruhn
a T-shirt	**ein T-Shirt**
	ien tee • shehrt
a toy	**ein Spielzeug**
	ien shpeel • tsoyg
copper	**Kupfer**
	koop • fehr
crystal	**Kristall**
	krihs • tahl
diamonds	**Diamanten**
	dee • ah • mahn • tuhn
white/yellow gold	**Weißgold/Gelbgold**
	vies • gohlt/gehlb • gohlt
pearls	**Perlen**
	pehr • luhn
pewter	**Zinn**
	tsihn
platinum	**Platin**
	plah • teen
sterling silver	**Sterlingsilber**
	shtehr • leeng • zihl • behr
Is this real?	**Ist das echt?**
	ihst dahs ehkht

Can you engrave it? **Können Sie etwas eingravieren?**
ker • _nuhn zee_ _eht_ • _vahs_
ien • _grah_ • _vee_ • _ruhn_

One of Germany's most famous products is the
Black Forest cuckoo clock. Though very expensive, these
clocks will last for generations if properly cared for. Another
popular and less expensive souvenir is a traditional German
beer stein. Collector beer steins are made from clay, glass
or pewter and can be brightly painted, with or without a lid
and engraved. Germany is also known for its toys: wooden
figurines, porcelain dolls and model trains. Other souvenirs
include: **lederhosen** (traditional German pants), lace and
porcelain.

SPORT & LEISURE

NEED TO KNOW

When's the game?	**Wann findet das Spiel statt?**
	vahn fihnd • uht dahs shpeel shtaht
Where's…?	**Wo ist … ?**
	voh ihst …
the beach	**der Strand**
	dehr shtrahnd
the park	**der Park**
	dehr pahrk
the pool	**der Pool**
	dehr pool
Is it safe to swim here?	**Kann man hier schwimmen?**
	kahn mahn heer shvihm • uhn
Can I hire golf clubs?	**Kann ich Golfschläger ausleihen?**
	kahn eekh gohlf • shlelig • ehr ows • lie • uhn
How much per hour?	**Wie viel kostet es pro Stunde?**
	vee feel kohs • tuht ehs proh shtoond • uh
How far is it to…?	**Wie weit ist es bis zum m /zur f …?**
	vee viet ihst ehs bihs tsoom /tsoor …
Show me on the map, please.	**Zeigen Sie es mir bitte auf dem Stadtplan.**
	tsieg • uhn zee ehs meer biht • tuh owf dehm shtaht • plahn

WATCHING SPORT

When's...?	**Wann findet ... statt?**
	vahn <u>fihnd</u> • uht ... shtaht
the baseball game	**das Baseballspiel**
	dahs <u>behs</u> • bahl • shpeel
the basketball game	**das Basketballspiel**
	dahs <u>bahs</u> • kuht • bahl • shpeel
the boxing match	**der Boxkampf**
	dehr <u>bohx</u> • kahmpf
the cricket match	**das Cricket-Turnier**
	dahs <u>krih</u> • kuht • toor • neer
the cycling race	**das Radrennen**
	dahs <u>rahd</u> • rehn • uhn
the golf tournament	**das Golfturnier**
	dahs <u>gohlf</u> • toor • neer
the soccer [football] game	**das Fußballspiel**
	dahs <u>foos</u> • bahl • shpeel
the tennis match	**das Tennismatch**
	dahs <u>tehn</u> • ihs • mahch
the volleyball game	**das Volleyballspiel**
	dahs <u>voh</u> • lee • bahl • shpeel
Who's playing?	**Wer spielt?**
	vehr shpeelt

Where's the racetrack/stadium?	**Wo ist die Rennbahn/das Stadion?** *voh ihst dee <u>rehn</u>•bahn/dahs <u>shtah</u>•dyohn*
Where can I place a bet?	**Wo kann ich eine Wette abschließen?** *voh kahn eekh <u>ien</u>•uh <u>veh</u>•tuh <u>ahp</u>•shlees•uhn*

For Tickets, see page 47.

Germany's most popular sport is **Fußball** (soccer); in fact, Germany has won the World Cup three times. Tennis is another popular sport; the German Tennis Federation boasts membership of more than one million. Other popular sports include biking, hiking, handball, basketball, volleyball, ice hockey, golf and horseback riding.
Casinos are found throughout Germany. The spa towns, in particular, are home to well-known casinos.

PLAYING SPORT

Where is/are…?	**Wo ist/sind …?** *voh ihst/zihnt …*
the golf course	**der Golfplatz** *dehr <u>gohlf</u>•plahts*
the gym	**die Sporthalle** *dee <u>shpohrt</u>•hah•luh*
the park	**der Park** *dehr pahrk*
the tennis courts	**die Tennisplätze** *dee <u>tehn</u>•ihs•pleht•suh*
How much per…?	**Wie viel kostet es pro …?** *vee feel <u>kohs</u>•tuht ehs proh …*

day	**Tag**	
	tak	
hour	**Stunde**	
	shtoond • uh	
game	**Spiel**	
	shpeel	
round	**Runde**	
	roond • uh	
Can I rent [hire]…?	**Kann ich … ausleihen?**	
	kahn eekh … ows • lie • huhn	
golf clubs	**Golfschläger**	
	gohlf • shlehg • ehr	
equipment	**eine Ausrüstung**	
	ien • uh ows • rews • toong	
a racket	**einen Schläger**	
	ien • uhn shlehg • ehr	

AT THE BEACH/POOL

Where's the beach/pool?	**Wo ist der Strand/Pool?**
	voh ihst dehr shtrahnt/pool
Is there a…?	**Gibt es einen …?**
	gihpt ehs ien • uhn …
kiddie pool	**Pool für Kinder**
	pool fewr kihnd • ehr
indoor/outdoor pool	**Hallenbad/Freibad**
	hahl • ehn • baht/frie • baht
lifeguard	**Rettungsschwimmer**
	reht • oongs • shvihm • ehr
Is it safe to swim/dive?	**Ist es sicher zu schwimmen/tauchen?**
	ihst ehs sihk • hehr tsoo shvihm • uhn/towkh • uhn
Is it safe for children?	**Ist es kindgerecht?**
	ihst ehs kihnt • guh • rehkht

(i)

Germany's main beach areas are located along the North Sea and Baltic Sea coasts. There are numerous types of beaches in Germany, including family, adults-only and nude beaches. A few of the more popular areas include Sylt, known for its nude beaches; Büsum, an intimate small town with calm North Sea waters; Helgoland, a Frisian island in the North Sea; Heiligendamm, Germany's oldest seaside resort; Heringsdorf, on the island of Usedom; and Kühlungsborn and Warnemünde, located on the Baltic Sea.

I'd like to rent hire...	**Ich möchte gern ... ausleihen.**
	eekh <u>merkht</u> • uh gehrn ... <u>ows</u> • lie • uhn
a deck chair	**einen Liegestuhl**
	<u>ien</u> • uhn <u>leeg</u> • uh • shtoohl
diving equipment	**eine Tauchausrüstung**
	<u>ien</u> • uh <u>towkh</u> • ows • rew • stoong
a jet ski	**einen Jet Ski**
	<u>ien</u> • uhn djeht skee
a motorboat	**ein Motorboot**
	ien <u>moht</u> • ohr • boht
a rowboat	**ein Ruderboot**
	ien <u>rood</u> • ehr • boht
snorkeling equipment	**eine Schnorchelausrüstung**
	<u>ien</u> • uh <u>shnohr</u> • khehl • ows • rew • stoong
a surfboard	**ein Surfboard**
	ien <u>soorf</u> • bohrd
a towel	**ein Handtuch**
	ien <u>hahnd</u> • tookh
an umbrella	**einen Schirm**
	<u>ien</u> • uhn sheerm
water skis	**Wasserski**
	<u>vahs</u> • ehr • shee

a windsurfer	**ein Surfbrett**
	ien serf • breht
For...hours.	**Für ... Stunden.**
	fewr ... shtoond • uhn

WINTER SPORTS

A lift pass for a day/ five days, please.	**Einen Liftpass für einen Tag/fünf Tage, bitte.**
	ien • uhn lihft • pahs fewr ien • uhn tahk/ fewnf tahg • uh biht • tuh
I'd like to hire...	**Ich möchte gerne ... ausleihen.**
	eekh merkht • uh gehr • nuh ... ows • lie • uhn
boots	**Stiefel**
	shteef • uhl
a helmet	**einen Helm**
	ien • uhn hehlm
poles	**Stöcke**
	shterk • uh
skis	**Skier**
	skee • ehr
a snowboard	**ein Snowboard**
	ien snohw • bohrd

snowshoes	**Schneeschuhe**
	shneh • shoo • uh
These are too big/small.	**Diese sind zu groß/klein.**
	dee • zuh zihnt tsoo grohs/klien
Are there lessons?	**Kann man Stunden nehmen?**
	kahn mahn shtoond • uhn neh • muhn
I'm a beginner.	**Ich bin Anfänger.**
	eekh bihn ahn • fehng • ehr
I'm experienced.	**Ich bin erfahren.**
	eekh been ehr • fahr • uhn
A trail [piste] map, please.	**Bitte einen Pistenplan.**
	biht • tuh ien • uhn pees • tuhn • plahn

YOU MAY SEE... 👁

SCHLEPPLIFT	drag lift
SEILBAHN	cable car
SESSELLIFT	chair lift
ANFÄNGER	novice
FORTGESCHRITTENE	intermediate
KÖNNER	expert
PISTE GESCHLOSSEN	trail [piste] closed

ℹ

Winter offers plenty of opportunities for outdoor activity in Germany. Alpine skiing, snowboarding, cross-country skiing, ice skating, tobogganing and hiking are just some of the options available to winter travelers.

OUT IN THE COUNTRY

A map of…, please.	**Eine Karte …, bitte.**
	ien • uh kahrt • uh … biht • tuh
this region	**dieser Region**
	deez • uhr rehg • yohn
the walking routes	**mit Wanderrouten**
	miht vahnd • ehr • root • uhn
the bike routes	**mit Radrouten**
	miht rahd • root • uhn
the trails	**mit Wanderwegen**
	miht vahnd • ehr • veh • guhn
Is it…?	**Ist es …?**
	ihst ehs …
easy	**leicht**
	liekht
difficult	**schwierig**
	shveer • eeg
far	**weit**
	viet
steep	**steil**
	shtiel
How far is it to…?	**Wie weit ist es bis …?**
	vee viet ihst ehs bihs …

Show me on the map, please.	**Zeigen Sie es mir bitte auf der Karte.** _tsieg • uhn zee ehs meer biht • tuh owf dehr kahrt • uh_
I'm lost.	**Ich habe mich verlaufen.** _eekh hahb • uh meekh fehr • lowf • uhn_
Where's...?	**Wo ist ...?** _voh ihst ..._
the bridge	**die Brücke** _dee brew • kuh_
the cave	**die Höhle** _dee her • luh_
the canyon	**der Canyon** _dehr kahn • yohn_
the cliff	**die Klippe** _dee klih • puh_
the desert	**die Wüste?** _dee vews • tuh_
the farm	**der Bauernhof** _dehr bow • ehrn • hohf_
the field	**das Feld** _dahs fehld_
the forest	**der Wald** _dehr vahld_
the hill	**der Hügel** _dehr hew • gehl_
the lake	**der See** _dehr zeh_
the mountain	**der Berg** _dehr behrg_
the nature preserve	**das Naturschutzgebiet** _dahs nah • toor • shoots • guh • beet_
the viewpoint	**der Aussichtspunkt** _dehr ows • seekhts • poonkt_
the park	**der Park** _dehr pahrk_

the path	**der Pfad**
	dehr pfahd
the peak	**der Gipfel**
	dehr <u>gihp</u> • fuhl
the picnic area	**der Picknickplatz**
	dehr <u>pihk</u> • nihk • plahts
the pond	**der Teich**
	dehr tiekh
the ravine	**die Schlucht**
	dee shlookht
the river	**der Fluss**
	dehr floos
the sea	**das Meer**
	dahs mehr
the (hot) spring	**die (heiße) Quelle**
	dee (<u>hie</u> • suh) <u>kveh</u> • luh
the stream	**der Strom**
	dehr shtrom
the valley	**das Tal**
	dahs tahl
the village	**das Dorf**
	dahs dohrf
the vineyard	**das Weingut**
	dahs <u>vien</u> • goot
the waterfall	**der Wasserfall**
	dehr <u>vahs</u> • ehr • fahl

TRAVELING WITH CHILDREN

NEED TO KNOW

Is there a discount for kids?	**Gibt es Ermäßigung für Kinder?**
	gihpt ehs ehr • meh • see • goong fewr kihn • dehr
Can you recommend a babysitter?	**Können Sie einen Babysitter empfehlen?**
	kern • uhn zee ien • uhn beh • bee • siht • ehr ehm • pfeh • luhn
Do you have a child's seat/highchair?	**Haben Sie einen Kindersitz/Kinderstuhl?**
	hah • buhn zee ien • uhn kihnd • ehr • zihts/kihnd • ehr • shtoohl
Where can I change the baby?	**Wo kann ich das Baby wickeln?**
	voh kahn eekh dahs beh • bee vihk • uhln

OUT & ABOUT

Can you recommend something for kids?	**Können Sie etwas für Kinder empfehlen?** _kern • uhn zee eht • vahs fewr kihnd • ehr ehm • pfeh • luhn_
Where's...?	**Wo ist ...?** _voh ihst ..._
the amusement park	**der Vergnügungspark** _dehr fehrg • new • goongs • pahrk_
the arcade	**die Spielhalle?** _dee shpeel • hah • luh_
the kiddie [paddling] pool	**das Kinderbecken** _dahs kihnd • ehr • beh • kuhn_
the park	**der Park** _dehr pahrk_
the playground	**der Spielplatz** _dehr shpeel • plats_
the zoo	**der Zoo** _dehr tsoh_
Are kids allowed?	**Sind Kinder erlaubt?** _zihnt kihnd • ehr ehr • lowbt_

YOU MAY HEAR...

Wie süß! _vee zews_	How cute!
Wie heißt er m/**sie** f**?** _vee hiest ehr/zee_	What's his/her name?
Wie alt ist er m/**sie** f**?** _vee ahlt ihst ehr/zee_	How old is he/she?

Is it safe for kids?	**Ist es für Kinder geeignet?**
	ihst ehs fewr <u>kihnd</u> • ehr guh • <u>ieg</u> • nuht
Is it suitable for... year olds?	**Ist es für ... Jahre alte Kinder geeignet?**
	ihst ehs fewr ... <u>yah</u> • ruh <u>ahlt</u> • uh
	<u>kihnd</u> • ehr guh • <u>ieg</u> • nuht

For Numbers, see page 22.

BABY ESSENTIALS

Do you have...?	**Haben Sie ...?**
	<u>hah</u> • buhn zee ...
a baby bottle	**eine Babyflasche**
	<u>ien</u> • uh beh • bee • <u>flahsh</u> • uh
baby food	**Babynahrung**
	<u>beh</u> • bee • nahr • oong
baby wipes	**feuchte Babytücher**
	<u>foykh</u> • tuh <u>beh</u> • bee • tewkh • ehr
a car seat	**einen Kindersitz**
	<u>ien</u> • uhn <u>kihnd</u> • ehr • zihts
a children's menu/ portion	**ein Kindermenü/eine Kinderportion**
	<u>ien</u> • uhn <u>kihnd</u> • ehr • meh • new/<u>ien</u> • uh
	<u>kihnd</u> • ehr • pohrtz • yohn • uhn
a child's seat/ highchair	**einen Kindersitz/Kinderstuhl**
	<u>ien</u> • uhn <u>kihnd</u> • ehr • zihts/
	<u>kihnd</u> • ehr • shtoohl
a crib/cot	**ein Gitterbett/Kinderbett**
	ien <u>giht</u> • tehr • beht/<u>kihnd</u> • ehr • beht
diapers [nappies]	**Windeln**
	<u>vihnd</u> • uhln
formula [baby food]	**Babynahrung**
	<u>beh</u> • bee • nah • roong
a pacifier [dummy]	**einen Schnuller**
	<u>ien</u> • uhn <u>shnool</u> • ehr

a playpen	**einen Laufstall**
	ien • uhn <u>lowf</u> • shtahl
a stroller	**einen Kinderwagen**
	ien • uhn
[pushchair]	*<u>kihnd</u> • ehr • vahg • uhn*
Can I breastfeed	**Kann ich das Baby hier stillen?**
	kahn eekh
the baby here?	*dahs beh • bee heer <u>shtihl</u> • uhn*
Where can I	**Wo kann ich das Baby stillen/wickeln?**
breastfeed/change	*voh kahn eekh dahs <u>beh</u> • bee <u>shtihl</u> • uhn/*
the baby?	*<u>vihk</u> • uhln*

For Dining with Children, see page 172.

BABYSITTING

Can you recommend	**Können Sie einen Babysitter empfehlen?**
a babysitter?	*<u>kern</u> • uhn zee <u>ien</u> • uhn*
	<u>beh</u> • bee • siht • ehr ehm • <u>pfeh</u> • luhn
What is the cost?	**Was sind die Kosten?**
	vahs zihnt dee <u>kohs</u> • tuhn
I'll be back by...	**Ich bin um ... zurück.**
	eekh been oom ... tsoo • <u>rewk</u>
If you need to	**Ich bin unter ... zu erreichen.**
contact me, call...	*eekh been <u>oont</u> • ehr ... tsoo ehr • <u>riekh</u> • uhn*

For Time, see page 25.

OTHEKE

EMERGENCIES

NEED TO KNOW

Help!	**Hilfe!**
	hihlf • uh
Go away!	**Gehen Sie weg!**
	geh • uhn zee vehk
Stop, thief!	**Haltet den Dieb!**
	hahlt • uht dehn deeb
Get a doctor!	**Holen Sie einen Arzt!**
	hohl • uhn zee _ien_ • uhn ahrtst
Fire!	**Feuer!**
	foy • ehr
I'm lost.	**Ich habe mich verlaufen.**
	eekh _hahb_ • uh meekh fehr • _lowf_ • uhn
Can you help me?	**Können Sie mir helfen?**
	kern • uhn zee meer _hehlf_ • uhn

YOU MAY HEAR...

Füllen Sie dieses Formular aus.
fewl • uhn zee _deez_ • uhs
fohr • moo • _lahr_ ows

Fill out this form.

Ihren Ausweis, bitte.
eehr • uhn _ows_ • vies _biht_ • tuh

Your ID, please.

Wann/Wo ist es passiert?
vahn/voh ihst ehs _pah_ • seert

When/Where did it happen?

Wie sah er m/sie f aus?
vee zah ehr/zee ows

What does he/she look like?

POLICE

NEED TO KNOW

Call the police!	**Rufen Sie die Polizei!**
	roof • uhn zee dee poh • leet • sie
Where's the police station?	**Wo ist das Polizeirevier?**
	voh ihst dahs poh • leet • sie • ruh • veer
There was an accident/attack.	**Es gab einen Unfall/Überfall.**
	ehs gahb ien • uhn oon • fahl/ ewb • ehr • fahl
My child is missing.	**Mein Kind ist weg.**
	mien kihnt ihst vehk
I need an interpreter.	**Ich brauche einen Dolmetscher.**
	eekh browkh • uh ien • uhn dohl • mech • ehr
I need to contact my lawyer/make a phone call.	**Ich muss mit meinem Anwalt sprechen/ telefonieren.**
	eekh moos miht mien • uhm ahn • vahlt shpreh • khehn/ tehl • eh • fohn • eer • uhn
I'm innocent.	**Ich bin unschuldig.**
	eekh bihn oon • shoold • eekh

CRIME & LOST PROPERTY

I want to report...	**Ich möchte ... melden.**
	eekh merkht • uh ... mehld • uhn
a mugging	**einen Überfall**
	ien • uhn ewb • ehr • fahl
a rape	**eine Vergewaltigung**
	ien • uh fehr • guh • vahlt • ee • goong

ⓘ

In an emergency, dial: **110** for the police
112 for the fire brigade
115 for the ambulance

a theft	**einen Diebstahl**
	ien • uhn deeb • shtahl
I've been mugged	**Ich wurde überfallen**
	eekh voor • duh ewb • ehr • fahl • uhn
I've been robbed	**Ich wurde beraubt**
	eekh voor • duh beh • rowbt
I've lost…	**Ich habe … verloren.**
	eekh hahb • uh … fehr • lohr • uhn
…was stolen.	**… wurde gestohlen.**
	… voor • duh geh • shtohl • uhn
My backpack	**Mein Rucksack**
	mien rook • zahk
My bicycle	**Mein Fahrrad**
	mien fahr • ahd
My camera	**Meine Kamera**
	mien • uh kah • meh • rah
My (hire) car	**Mein Mietauto**
	mien meet • ow • toh
My computer	**Mein Computer**
	mien kohm • pjoo • tehr
My credit card	**Meine Kreditkarte**
	mien • uh kreh • deet • kahrt • uh
My jewelry	**Mein Schmuck**
	mien shmook
My money	**Mein Geld**
	mien gehlt
My passport	**Mein Reisepass**
	mien riez • uh • pahs

My purse [handbag]	**Meine Handtasche**
	mien • uh hahnd • tahsh • uh
My traveler's checks [cheques]	**Meine Reisechecks**
	mien • uh riez • uh • shehks
My wallet	**Meine Brieftasche**
	mien • uh breef • tahsh • uh
I need a police report.	**Ich brauche einen Polizeibericht.**
	eekh browkh • uh ien • uhn
	poh • leet • sie • beh • reekht
Where is the British/ American/Irish embassy?	**Wo ist die britische/amerikanische/ irische Botschaft?**
	voh ihst dee brih • tih • shuh/
	ah • meh • rih • kah • nih • shuh/
	eer • ih • shuh boht • shaft

HEALTH

NEED TO KNOW

I'm sick.	**Ich bin krank.**
	eekh bihn krahnk
I need an English-speaking doctor.	**Ich brauche einen englischsprechenden Arzt.**
	eekh browkh • uh ien • uhn
	ehng • glihsh • shprehkh • ehnd • uhn
	ahrtst
It hurts here.	**Es tut hier weh.**
	ehs toot heer veh
I have a stomachache.	**Ich habe Magenschmerzen.**
	eekh hahb • uh
	mahg • uhn • shmehrt • suhn

FINDING A DOCTOR

Can you recommend a doctor/dentist?	**Können Sie einen Arzt/Zahnarzt empfehlen?**
	kern • uhn zee ien • uhn ahrtst/ tsahn • ahrtst ehm • pfeh • luhn
Can the doctor come here?	**Kann der Arzt herkommen?**
	kahn dehr ahrtst hehr • kohm • uhn
I need an English-speaking doctor.	**Ich brauche einen englischsprechenden Arzt.**
	eekh browkh • uh ien • uhn ehng • gleesh • shprehkh • ehnd • uhn ahrtst
What are the office hours?	**Wann sind die Sprechstunden?**
	vahn zihnt dee shprekh • shtoond • uhn
It's urgent.	**Es ist dringend.**
	ehs ihst dreeng • uhnt
I'd like an appointment for…	**Ich möchte einen Termin für …**
	eekh merkht • uh ien • uhn tehr • meen fewr …
today	**heute**
	hoy • tuh
tomorrow	**morgen**
	mohr • guhn
as soon as possible	**so bald wie möglich**
	zoh bahld vee merg • leekh

SYMPTOMS

I'm bleeding.	**Ich blute.**
	eekh bloot • uh
I'm constipated.	**Ich habe Verstopfung.**
	eekh hahb • uh fehr • shtohpf • oong

I'm dizzy.	**Mir ist schwindlig.**	
	meer ihst <u>shvihnd</u> • leekh	
I'm nauseous.	**Mir ist schlecht.**	
	meer ihst shlehkht	
I'm vomiting.	**Ich übergebe mich.**	
	eekh ewb • ehr • <u>gehb</u> • uh meekh	
It hurts here.	**Es tut hier weh.**	
	ehs toot heer veh	
I have…	**Ich habe …**	
	eekh <u>hahb</u> • uh …	
an allergic reaction	**eine allergische Reaktion**	
	<u>ien</u> • uh ah • <u>lehr</u> • geesh • uh reh • ahk • <u>syon</u>	
chest pain	**Brustschmerzen**	
	<u>broost</u> • shmehrt • suhn	
cramps	**Krämpfe**	
	<u>krehmp</u> • fuh	
diarrhea	**Durchfall**	
	<u>doorkh</u> • fahl	
an earache	**Ohrenschmerzen**	
	<u>oht</u> • uhn • shmehrt • suhn	
a fever	**Fieber**	
	<u>feeb</u> • ehr	
pain	**Schmerzen**	
	<u>shmehrt</u> • suhn	
a rash	**einen Ausschlag**	
	<u>ien</u> • uhn <u>ows</u> • shlahg	
a sprain	**eine Verstauchung**	
	<u>ien</u> • uh fehr • <u>shtowkh</u> • oong	
some swelling	**eine Schwellung**	
	<u>ien</u> • uh <u>shvehl</u> • oong	
a sore throat	**Halsschmerzen**	
	<u>hahls</u> • shmehrt • suhn	
a stomachache	**Magenschmerzen**	
	<u>mahg</u> • uhn • shmehrt • suhn	

YOU MAY HEAR...

Was stimmt nicht mit Ihnen?
vahs shtihmt neekht miht <u>eehn</u> • uhn
What's wrong?

Wo tut es weh?
voh toot ehs veh
Where does it hurt?

Tut es hier weh?
toot ehs heer veh
Does it hurt here?

Nehmen Sie Medikamente?
<u>nehm</u> • uhn zee mehd • ee • kah • <u>mehnt</u> • uh
Are you on medication?

Sind Sie auf irgendetwas allergisch?
zihnt zee owf eer • <u>guhnd</u> • <u>eht</u> • vahs
ah • <u>lehr</u> • geesh
Are you allergic to anything? anything?

Öffnen Sie Ihren Mund.
<u>erf</u> • nuhn zee <u>eehr</u> • uhn moont
Open your mouth.

Tief einatmen.
teef ien • <u>aht</u> • muhn
Breathe deeply.

Bitte husten.
<u>biht</u> • tuh <u>hoos</u> • tuhn
Cough, please.

Gehen Sie ins Krankenhaus.
<u>geh</u> • uhn zee ihns <u>krahnk</u> • uhn • hows
Go to the hospital.

Es ist ...
ehs ihst ...
It's...

  gebrochen
  geh • <u>brohkh</u> • uhn
broken

  ansteckend
  <u>ahn</u> • shtehk • uhnt
contagious

  infiziert
  een • fee • <u>tseert</u>
infected

  verstaucht
  fehr • <u>shtowkht</u>
sprained

  nichts Ernstes
  neekhts <u>ehrnst</u> • uhs
nothing serious

sunstroke	**einen Sonnenstich**
	ien • uhn zohn • uhn • shteekh
I've been sick [ill] for...days.	**Ich bin seit ... Tagen krank.**
	eekh bihn ziet ... <u>tahg</u> • uhn krahnk

CONDITIONS

I'm...	**Ich bin ...**
	eekh bihn ...
anemic	**anämisch**
	ah • <u>nay</u> • meesh
asthmatic	**Asthmatiker**
	ahst • <u>maht</u> • eek • ehr
diabetic	**Diabetiker**
	dee • ah • <u>beht</u> • eek • her
epileptic	**Epileptiker/Epileptikerin**
	eh • pih • lehp • tih • kuhr/
	eh • pih • lehp • tih • kuh • rihn
I'm allergic to antibiotics/ penicillin.	**Ich bin allergisch auf Antibiotika/ Penicillin.**
	eekh bihn <u>ah</u> • lehrg • eesh owf
	ahn • tee • bee • <u>oh</u> • tee • kah/
	peh • nih • <u>sihl</u> • ihn
I have...	**Ich habe ...**
	eekh <u>hahb</u> • uh ...
arthritis	**Arthritis**
	<u>ahr</u> • tree • tihs
a heart condition	**eine Herzkrankheit**
	<u>ien</u> • uh <u>hehrts</u> • krahnk • hiet
high/low blood pressure	**hohen/niedrigen Blutdruck**
	<u>hoh</u> • uhn/<u>need</u> • ree • gehn <u>bloot</u> • drook
I'm on...	**Ich nehme ...**
	eekh <u>nehm</u> • uh ...

For Meals & Cooking, see page 175.

TREATMENT

Do I need a prescription/ medicine?	**Brauche ich ein Rezept/Medikament?** *browkh • uh eekh ien reh • tsehpt/ mehd • ee • kah • mehnt*
Can you prescribe a generic drug? [unbranded medication]	**Können Sie ein ähnliches, günstiges Medikament verschreiben?** *kern • uhn zee ien ehn • lee • khehs gewn • stee • guhs meh • dee • kah • mehnt fehr • shrieb • uhn*
Where can I get it?	**Wo kann ich es bekommen?** *voh kahn eekh ehs buh • kohm • uhn*
Is this over the counter?	**Ist es rezeptfrei?** *ihst ehs reh • tsehpt • frie*

HOSPITAL

Notify my family, please.	**Bitte benachrichtigen Sie meine Familie.** *biht • tuh buh • nahkh • reekh • tih • guhn zee mien • uh fah • mee • lee • uh*
I'm in pain.	**Ich habe Schmerzen.** *eekh hahb • uh shmehrt • suhn*
I need a doctor/nurse.	**Ich brauche einen Arzt/eine Schwester.** *eekh browkh • uh ien • uhn ahrtst/ien • uh shvehs • tehr*
When are visiting hours?	**Wann ist die Besuchszeit?** *vahn ihst dee beh • zookhs • tsiet*
I'm visiting…	**Ich besuche …** *eekh beh • zookh • uh …*

DENTIST

I have…	**Ich habe …** *eekh hahb • uh …*

a broken tooth	**einen kaputten Zahn**
	ien • _uhn kah_ • _poot_ • _uhn tsahn_
a lost filling	**eine Füllung verloren**
	ien • _uh fewl_ • _oong fehr_ • _lohr_ • _uhn_
a toothache	**Zahnschmerzen**
	tsahn • _shmehrts_ • _uhn_
Can you fix this denture?	**Können Sie diese Prothese reparieren?**
	kern • _uhn zee_ _deez_ • _uh proh_ • _teh_ • _zuh_
	reh • _pah_ • _reer_ • _uhn_

For What to Take, see page 155.

GYNECOLOGIST

I have cramps/ a vaginal infection.	**Ich habe Krämpfe/eine Scheideninfektion.**
	eekh _hahb_ • _uh_ _krehmp_ • _fuh/ie_ • _nuh_
	shnied • _uhn_ • _ihn_ • _fehk_ • _tyohn_
I missed my period.	**Meine Periode ist ausgeblieben.**
	mien • _uh pehr_ • _yoh_ • _duh ihst_
	ows • _geh_ • _bleeb_ • _uhn_
I'm on the Pill.	**Ich nehme die Pille.**
	eekh _nehm_ • _uh dee_ _pihl_ • _uh_
I'm (one/two/three/ four/five/six/seven/ eight/nine months) pregnant.	**Ich bin (im ersten/zweiten/dritten/ vierten/fünften/sechsten/siebten/ achten/neunten Monat) schwanger.**
	eekh bihn (ihm ehrs • _thun/ tsvai_ • _thun/_
	dree • _thun/feer_ • _thun/ewnf_ • _thun/_
	sehks • _thun/seeb_ • _thun/ahkh_ • _thun/_
	noyn • _thun moh_ • _naht) shvahn_ • _guhr_
I'm not pregnant.	**Ich bin nicht schwanger.**
	eekh bihn (neekht) _shvahng_ • _ehr_
My last period was...	**Meine letzte Periode war ...**
	mien • _uh lehts_ • _uh pehr_ • _yohd_ • _uh vahr ..._

OPTICIAN

I've lost…	**Ich habe … verloren.** *eekh hahb • uh … fehr • lohr • uhn*
a contact lens	**eine Kontaktlinse** *ien • uh kohn • tahkt • lihnz • uh*
my glasses	**meine Brille** *mien • uh brihl • uh*
a lens	**ein Brillenglas** *ien brihl • uhn • glahs*

PAYMENT & INSURANCE

How much?	**Wie viel kostet es?** *vee feel kohs • tuht ehs*
Can I pay by credit card?	**Kann ich mit Kreditkarte bezahlen?** *kahn eekh miht kreh • deet • kahr • tuh beht • sahl • uhn*
I have insurance.	**Ich bin versichert.** *eekh bihn fehr • zeekh • ehrt*
I need a receipt for my insurance.	**Ich brauche eine Quittung für meine Versicherung.** *eekh browkh • uh ien • uh kviht • oong fewr mien • uh fehr • zeekh • ehr • oong*

PHARMACY

NEED TO KNOW

Where's the pharmacy?	**Wo ist die Apotheke?**
	voh ihst dee ah • poh • <u>tehk</u> • uh
What time does it open/close?	**Wann öffnet/schließt sie?**
	vahn <u>erf</u> • nuht/shleest zee
What would you recommend for…?	**Was empfehlen Sie bei …?**
	vahs ehm • <u>pfeh</u> • luhn zee bie …
How much do I take?	**Wie viel muss ich einnehmen?**
	vee feel moos eekh ei • <u>nehm</u> • uhn

WHAT TO TAKE

How much do I take?	**Wie viel muss ich einnehmen?**
	vee feel moos eekh <u>ien</u> • nehm • uhn
How often?	**Wie oft?**
	vee ohft
Is it safe for children?	**Ist es für Kinder geeignet?**
	ihst ehs fewr <u>kihnd</u> • ehr geh • <u>ieg</u> • nuht
I'm taking…	**Ich nehme …**
	eekh <u>neh</u> • muh …
Are there side effects?	**Gibt es Nebenwirkungen?**
	gihpt ehs <u>nehb</u> • uhn • veerk • oong • uhn
I need something for…	**Ich brauche etwas gegen …**
	ihkh <u>browkh</u> • uh <u>eht</u> • vahs <u>geh</u> • guhn …
a cold	**eine Erkältung**
	<u>ien</u> • uh ehr • <u>kehlt</u> • oong
a cough	**Husten**
	<u>hoos</u> • tuhn

diarrhea	**Durchfall**
	doorkh • fahl
a headache	**Kopfschmerzen**
	kohpf • shmehr • tsuhn
insect bites	**Insektenstiche**
	een • _zehkt_ • uhn • shteekh • uh
motion [travel]	**die Reisekrankheit**
sickness	dee _riez_ • uh • krahnk • hiet
a sore throat	**Halsschmerzen**
	hahls • shmehrt • suhn
sunburn	**Sonnenbrand**
	zohn • uhn • brahnt
a toothache	**Zahnschmerzen**
	tsahn • shmehr • tsuhn
an upset stomach	**eine Magenverstimmung**
	ien • uh _mahg_ • uhn • fehr • shtihm • oong

YOU MAY HEAR…

EINMAL/DREIMAL AM TAG	once/three times a day
TABLETTE	tablet
TROPFEN	drop
TEELÖFFEL	teaspoon
NACH/VOR/MIT DEN MAHLZEITEN	after/before/with meals
AUF LEEREN MAGEN	on an empty stomach
IM GANZEN SCHLUCKEN	swallow whole
KANN BENOMMENHEIT VERURSACHEN	may cause drowsiness
NUR ZÜR ÄUSSEREN ANWENDUNG	for external use only

ⓘ

In Germany, there is a distinction between **Apotheke** (pharmacy) and **Drogerie** (drugstore).
Die Apotheke, usually featuring a large red A sign, dispenses prescription and over-the-counter medication. **Die Drogerie** sells toiletries and other personal items. Pharmacies are open 9:00 a.m. to 6:30 p.m. Monday to Friday, and from 9:00 a.m. to 1:00 p.m. (sometimes 4:00 p.m) on Saturday. Most large cities and towns have at least one 24-hour pharmacy. Closed pharmacies will have a sign on the door indicating the nearest 24-hour location.

BASIC SUPPLIES

I'd like…	**Ich hätte gern …** *eekh heh • tuh gehrn …*
acetaminophen [paracetamol]	**Paracetamol** *pah • rah • seht • ah • mohl*
antiseptic cream	**eine antiseptische Creme** *ahn • tee • zehp • tee • shuh krehm*
aspirin	**Aspirin** *ahs • pih • reen*
bandages	**Pflaster** *pflahs • tehr*
a comb	**einen Kamm** *ien • uhn kahm*
condoms	**Kondome** *kohn • dohm • uh*
contact lens solution	**Kontaktlinsenlösung** *kohn • tahkt • lehnz • uhn • lerz • oong*
deodorant	**Deodorant** *deh • oh • doh • rahnt*

a hairbrush	**eine Haarbürste**
	ien • uh _hahr_ • bewr • stuh
hairspray	**Haarspray**
	hahr • shpraye
ibuprofen	**Ibuprofen**
	ee • boo • proh • _fuhn_
insect repellent	**Insektenspray**
	ihn • _zehkt_ • uhn • shpray
lotion	**Lotion**
	loht • _syohn_
a nail file	**eine Nagelfeile**
	ien • uh _nahg_ • ehl • fie • luh
a (disposable) razor	**(Wegwerf-) Rasierer**
	vehk • vehrf rah • _zeer_ • ehr
razor blades	**Rasierklingen**
	rah • _zeer_ • kleeng • uhn
rubbing alcohol	**Franzbranntwein**
[surgical spirit]	_frahnts_ • brahnt • vien
sanitary napkins	**Monatsbinden**
[towels]	_moh_ • nahts • bihnd • uhn
shampoo/	**Shampoo/Spülung**
conditioner	_shahm_ • poo/_shpewl_ • oong
soap	**Seife**
	zie • fuh
sunscreen	**Sonnenmilch**
	zohn • nuhn • mihlkh
tampons	**Tampons**
	tahm • pohns
tissues	**Taschentücher**
	tahsh • uhn • tewkh • ehr
toilet paper	**Toilettenpapier**
	toy • _leht_ • uhn • pah • peer
toothpaste	**Zahnpasta**
	tsahn • pahs • tah

For Baby Essentials, see page 140.

CHILD HEALTH & EMERGENCY

Can you recommend a pediatrician?	**Können Sie einen Kinderarzt empfehlen?**
	kern • uhn zee <u>ien</u> • uhn <u>kihnd</u> • ehr • ahrtst ehm • <u>pfeh</u> • luhn
My child is allergic to…	**Mein Kind ist allergisch auf …**
	mien kihnt ihst ah • <u>lehrg</u> • eesh owf …
My child is missing.	**Mein Kind ist weg.**
	mien kihnt ihst vehk
Have you seen a boy/girl?	**Haben Sie einen Jungen/ein Mädchen gesehen?**
	hah • buhn zee <u>icn</u> • uhn <u>yoong</u> • uhn/ien meht • khuhn guh • <u>zeh</u> • uhn

For Police, see page 145.

DISABLED TRAVELERS

NEED TO KNOW

Is there...?	**Gibt es ...?**
	gihpt ehs ...
access for the disabled	**einen Zugang für Behinderte**
	ien • uhn tsoo • gahng fewr beh • hihnd • ehrt • uh
a wheelchair ramp	**eine Rollstuhlrampe**
	ien • uh rohl • shtool • rahm • puh
a disabled-accessible toilet	**eine Behindertentoilette**
	ien • uh beh • hihn • dehrt • uhn • toy • leh • tuh
I need...	**Ich brauche ...**
	eekh browkh • uh ...
assistance	**Hilfe**
	hihlf • uh
an elevator [a lift]	**einen Fahrstuhl**
	ien • uhn fahr • shtoohl
a ground-floor room	**ein Zimmer im Erdgeschoss**
	ien tsihm • ehr ihm ehrd • guh • shohs

ASKING FOR ASSISTANCE

I'm...	**Ich bin ...**
	eekh bihn ...
disabled	**behindert**
	beh • hihn • dehrt
visually impaired	**sehbehindert**
	zeh • buh • hihn • dehrt

hearing impaired/	**hörgeschädigt/taub**
deaf	*her • guh • sheh • deegt/towb*
I'm unable to walk	**Ich kann nicht weit laufen/die Treppe**
far/use the stairs.	**benutzen.**
	eekh kahn neekht viet <u>low</u> • fuhn/dee
	<u>trehp</u> • uh beh • <u>noot</u> • suhn
Please speak louder.	**Bitte sprechen Sie lauter.**
	biht • tuh <u>shprehkh</u> • uhn zee <u>lowt</u> • ehr
Can I bring my	**Kann ich meinen Rollstuhl mitbringen?**
wheelchair?	*kahn eekh <u>mien</u> • uhn <u>rohl</u> • shtoohl*
	<u>miht</u> • brihng • uhn
Are guide dogs	**Sind Blindenhunde erlaubt?**
permitted?	*zihnt <u>blihnd</u> • uhn • hoond • uh ehr • <u>lowbt</u>*
Can you help me?	**Können Sie mir helfen?**
	kern • uhn zee meer <u>hehlf</u> • uhn
Please open/hold	**Bitte öffnen/halten Sie die Tür.**
the door.	*<u>biht</u> • tuh erf • nuhn/<u>hahlt</u> • uhn zee dee tewr*

For Health, see page 147.

FOOD & DRINK

EATING OUT

NEED TO KNOW

Can you recommend a good restaurant/ bar?	**Können Sie ein gutes Restaurant/ eine gute Bar empfehlen?** _ker • nuhn zee ien <u>goo</u> • tuhs reh • stow • <u>rahnt</u>/ien • uh goo • tuh bahr ehm • <u>pfeh</u> • luhn_
Is there a traditional German/an inexpensive restaurant nearby?	**Gibt es in der Nähe ein typisch deutsches/preisgünstiges Restaurant?** _gihpt ehs ihn dehr <u>neh</u> • uh ien <u>tew</u> • peesh <u>doy</u> • chuhs/ <u>pries</u> • gewn • stee • guhs reh • stow • <u>rahnt</u>_
A table for…, please.	**Bitte einen Tisch für …** _<u>biht</u> • tuh ien • uhn tihsh fewr …_
Can we sit…?	**Können wir … sitzen?** _<u>ker</u> • nuhn veer … <u>ziht</u> • tsuhn_
here/there	**hier/dort** _heer/dohrt_
outside	**draußen** _<u>drow</u> • suhn_
in a non-smoking area	**in einem Nichtraucherbereich** _ihn <u>ien</u> • uhm neekht • <u>row</u> • khehr • beh • riehk_
I'm waiting for someone.	**Ich warte auf jemanden.** _eekh <u>vahr</u> • tuh owf <u>yeh</u> • mahnd • uhn_
Where are the toilets?	**Wo ist die Toilette?** _voh ihst dee toy • <u>leh</u> • tuh_

A menu, please.	**Die Speisekarte, bitte.**
	dee <u>shpie</u> • zuh • kahr • tuh <u>biht</u> • tuh
What do you recommend?	**Was empfehlen Sie?**
	vahs ehm • <u>pfeh</u> • luhn zee
I'd like…	**Ich möchte …**
	eekh merkh • tuh …
Some more…, please.	**Etwas mehr …, bitte.**
	<u>eht</u> • vahs mehr … <u>biht</u> • tuh
Enjoy your meal!	**Guten Appetit!**
	<u>goo</u> • tuhn ah • puh • <u>teet</u>
The check [bill], please.	**Die Rechnung, bitte.**
	dee <u>rehkh</u> • noonk <u>biht</u> • tuh
Is service included?	**Ist die Bedienung im Preis enthalten?**
	ihsht dee buh • <u>dee</u> • nung ihm pries ehnt • hahl • tuhn
Can I pay by credit card/have a receipt?	**Kann ich mit Kreditkarte bezahlen/ eine Quittung haben?**
	kahn eekh miht kreh • <u>deet</u> • kahr • tuh beht • sahl • uhn/ien • uh kvee • toonk <u>hah</u> • buhn
Thank you!	**Danke!**
	<u>dahn</u> • kuh

WHERE TO EAT

Can you recommend…?	**Können Sie … empfehlen?**
	<u>ker</u> • nuhn zee … ehm • <u>pfeh</u> • luhn
a restaurant	**ein Restaurant**
	ien reh • stow • <u>rahnt</u>
a bar	**eine Bar**
	ien • uh bahr

a cafe	**ein Café**
	ien kah • feh
a fast-food place	**ein Schnellrestaurant**
	ien shnehl • reh • stow • rahnt
a snack bar	**einen Imbiss**
	ien • uhn ihm • bees
a cheap restaurant	**ein billiges Restaurant**
	ien bihl • lee • guhs reh • stow • rahnt
an expensive restaurant	**ein teures Restaurant**
	ien toy • rehs reh • stow • rahnt
a restaurant with a good view	**ein Restaurant mit schöner Aussicht**
	ien reh • stow • rahnt miht sher • nuhr ows • seekht
an authentic/ a non-touristy restaurant	**ein authentisches/ein nicht so touristisches Restaurant**
	ien ow • tehn • tih • shuhs/ien neekht zoh tou • rihs • tih • shuhs reh • stow • rahnt

RESERVATIONS & PREFERENCES

I'd like to reserve a table...	**Ich möchte einen Tisch ... reservieren**
	eekh merkh • tuh ien • uhn tihsh ... reh • zuh • veer • ehn
for two	**für zwei Personen**
	fewr tsvie pehr • zohn • uhn
for this evening	**für heute Abend**
	fewr hoy • tuh ah • behnt
for tomorrow at...	**für morgen um ...**
	fewr mohr • guhn oom ...
A table for two, please.	**Bitte einen Tisch für zwei.**
	biht • tuh ien • uhn tihsh fewr tsvie
We have a reservation.	**Wir haben eine Reservierung.**
	veer hah • buhn ien • uh reh • zuh • veer • uhng

My name is...	**Mein Name ist ...**
	mien <u>nahm</u> • uh ihst ...
Can we sit...?	**Können wir ... sitzen?**
	<u>ker</u> • nuhn veer ... <u>ziht</u> • tsuhn
here/there	**hier/dort**
	heer/dohrt
outside	**draußen**
	<u>drow</u> • suhn
in a non-smoking area	**in einem Nichtraucherbereich**
	ihn <u>ien</u> • uhm
	<u>neekht</u> • row • khuhr • beh • riekh
by the window	**am Fenster**
	ahm <u>fehn</u> • stehr
in the shade	**im Schatten**
	ihm shaht • tehn

YOU MAY HEAR...

Haben Sie eine Reservierung?	Do you have a reservation?
<u>hah</u> • buhn zee <u>ien</u> • uh	
reh • zuh • <u>veer</u> • uhng	
Für wie viele Personen?	For how many people?
fewr vee <u>fee</u> • luh pehr • <u>zohn</u> • uhn	
Raucher oder Nichtraucher?	Smoking or non-smoking?
<u>row</u> • khuhr <u>oh</u> • duhr <u>neekht</u> • row • khuhr	
Möchten Sie jetzt bestellen?	Are you ready to order?
<u>merkh</u> • tuhn zee yehtst buh • <u>shteh</u> • luhn	
Was möchten Sie?	What would you like?
vahs <u>merkh</u> • tuhn zee	
Ich empfehle...	I recommend...
eekh ehm • <u>pfeh</u> • luh ...	
Guten Appetit.	Enjoy your meal.
<u>goo</u> • tuhn ah • puh • <u>teet</u>	

in the sun	**in der Sonne**
	ihn dehr sohn • nuh
Where are the toilets?	**Wo ist die Toilette?**
	voh ihst dee toy • leh • tuh

HOW TO ORDER

Waiter/Waitress!	**Bedienung!**
	buh • dee • nounk
We're ready to order.	**Wir möchten bitte bestellen.**
	weer merkh • tuhn biht • tuh buh • shteh • luhn
May I see the wine list, please?	**Die Weinkarte, bitte.**
	dee vien • kahr • tuh biht • tuh
I'd like…	**Ich möchte …**
	eekh merhk • tuh …
a bottle of…	**eine Flasche …**
	ien • uh flah • shuh …
a carafe of…	**eine Karaffe …**
	ien • uh kah • rah • fuh …
a glass of…	**ein Glas …**
	ien glahs …
The menu, please.	**Die Speisekarte, bitte.**
	dee shpie • zuh • kahr • tuh biht • tuh
Do you have…?	**Haben Sie …?**
	hah • buhn zee …
a menu in English	**eine Speisekarte in Englisch**
	ien • uh shpie • zuh • kahr • tuh ihn ehn • gleesh
a fixed-price menu	**ein Festpreismenü**
	ien fehst • pries • meh • new
a children's menu	**ein Kindermenü**
	ien kihn • dehr • meh • new
What do you recommend?	**Was empfehlen Sie?**
	vahs ehm • pfeh • luhn zee

What's this?	**Was ist das?**
	vahs ihsht dahs
What's in it?	**Was ist darin?**
	vahs ihsht dah • <u>rihn</u>
Is it spicy?	**Ist es scharf?**
	ihsht ehs shahrf
I'd like…	**Ich möchte gern …**
	eekh <u>merkh</u> • tuh gehrn …
More…, please.	**Mehr …, bitte.**
	mehr … <u>biht</u> • tuh
With/Without…	**Mit/Ohne …**
	miht/<u>oh</u> • nuh …
I can't eat…	**Ich vertrage kein/keine …**
	eekh fehr • <u>trah</u> • guh kien/<u>kien</u> • uh …
rare	**roh**
	roh
medium	**medium**
	<u>meh</u> • dee • uhm
well-done	**durchgebraten**
	<u>doorkh</u> • geh • brah • tuhn
Without…, please.	**Ohne …, bitte.**
	<u>oh</u> • nuh … <u>biht</u> • tuh
It's to go [take away], please.	**Bitte zum Mitnehmen.**
	<u>biht</u> • tuh tsoom <u>miht</u> • neh • muhn

For Drinks, see page 193.

YOU MAY SEE…

SPEISEKARTE	menu
TAGESMENÜ	menu of the day
SPEZIALITÄTEN	specials

beere 4,5%
Drachenblut 12,5%
Met (Honigwein) 12%
Punsch (Glühwein) 9%
Schokolade 0%
Kinderpunsch 0%

COOKING METHODS

baked	**gebacken**
	guh • bahkh • uhn
boiled	**gekocht**
	guh • kohkht
braised	**geschmort**
	guh • shmohrt
breaded	**paniert**
	pah • neert
creamed	**püriert**
	pew • reert
diced	**gewürfelt**
	guh • vewr • fuhlt
filleted	**filetiert**
	fee • luh • teert
fried	**gebraten**
	guh • brah • tuhn
grilled	**gegrillt**
	guh • grihlt
poached	**pochiert**
	poh • sheert
roasted	**geröstet**
	guh • rer • stuht

sautéed	**sautiert**
	zow • teert
smoked	**geräuchert**
	guh • _roy_ • khuhrt
steamed	**gedünstet**
	guh • _dewn_ • stuht
stewed	**geschmort**
	guh • _shmohrt_
stuffed	**gefüllt**
	guh • _fewlt_

DIETARY REQUIREMENTS

I'm...	**Ich bin ...**
	eekh bihn ...
diabetic	**Diabetiker**
	dee • ah • _beh_ • tee • kehr
lactose intolerant	**laktoseintolerant**
	lahk • thoh • suh • een • tho • luh • rahnt
vegetarian	**Vegetarier**
	veh • guh • _tah_ • ree • ehr
vegan	**Veganer**
	veh • gah • nehr
I'm allergic to...	**Ich bin allergisch auf ...**
	eekh bihn ah • _lehr_ • geesh owf ...
I can't eat...	**Ich kann ... essen.**
	eekh kahn ... _eh_ • zuhn
dairy products	**keine Milchprodukte**
	kien • uh _meelkh_ • proh • dook • tuh
gluten	**kein Gluten**
	kien _gloo_ • tuhn
nuts	**keine Nüsse**
	kien • uh _new_ • suh
pork	**kein Schweinefleisch**
	kien _shvie_ • nuh • fliesh

shellfish	**keine Schalentiere**
	kien • uh shah • luhn • tee • ruh
spicy foods	**keine scharf gewürzten Speisen**
	kien • uh shahrf guh • vewrt • stuhn
	shpie • zuhn
wheat	**kein Weizen**
	kien vie • tsuhn
Is it halal/kosher?	**Ist es halal/koscher?**
	ihsht ehs hah • lahl/koh • shuhr
Do you have...?	**Haben Sie...?**
	hah • buhn zee
skimmed milk	**Magermilch**
	mah • guhr • meelkh
whole milk	**Vollmilch**
	foll • meelkh
soya milk	**Sojamilch**
	soh • yah • meelkh

DINING WITH CHILDREN

Do you have children's portions?	**Haben Sie Kinderportionen?**
	hah • buhn zee
	kihn • dehr • pohr • syoh • nuhn
Can I have a highchair/child's seat?	**Einen Kindersitz/Kinderstuhl, bitte.**
	ien • uhn kihnd • ehr • zihtz/
	kihn • dehr • shtuhl biht • tuh
Where can I feed/change the baby?	**Wo kann ich das Baby füttern/wickeln?**
	voh kahn eekh dahs beh • bee few • tuhrn/
	vihk • uhln
Can you warm this?	**Können Sie das warm machen?**
	ker • nuhn zee dahs vahrm mah • khuhn

For Traveling with Children, see page 138.

HOW TO COMPLAIN

When will our food be ready?
Wie lange dauert es noch mit dem Essen?
vee lahng • uh dow • ehrt ehs nohkh miht dehm eh • suhn

We can't wait any longer.
Wir können nicht mehr länger warten.
veer ker • nuhn neekht mehr lehng • ehr vahr • tuhn

We're leaving.
Wir gehen jetzt.
veer geh • ehn yehtst

I didn't order this.
Das habe ich nicht bestellt.
dahs hah • buh eekh neekht buh • shtehlt

I ordered…
Ich habe … bestellt.
eekh hah • buh … buh • shtehlt

I can't eat this.
Ich kann das nicht essen.
eekh kahn dahs neekht eh • suhn

This is too…
Das ist zu …
dahs ihsht tsoo …

cold/hot
kalt/heiß
kahlt/hies

salty/spicy
salzig/scharf gewürzt
sahl • tseek/shahrf guh • vewrts

tough/bland
zäh/fad
tseh/fahd

This isn't clean/fresh.
Das ist nicht sauber/frisch.
dahs ihsht neekht zow • buhr/frihsh

> ⓘ
>
> Service is included in the bill in German restaurants and bars, as is value added tax (VAT). However, it is still typical to give a small tip, rounding up to the nearest euro or two for a small bill or adding 5-10% for a bigger bill. Note that it is not usual to be given an actual check [bill]. Instead, the server will just tell you what your total is and you hand them the money, specifying how much change you would like to have back, allowing for the tip you want to give.

PAYING

The check [bill], please.	**Die Rechnung, bitte.** *dee rehkh • noonk biht • tuh*
Separate checks [bills], please.	**Getrennte Rechnungen, bitte.** *geh • trehn • tuh rehkh • noong • uhn biht • tuh*
It's all together.	**Alles zusammen.** *ah • luhs tsoo • zah • muhn*
Is service included?	**Ist die Bedienung im Preis enthalten?** *ihsht dee buh • dee • noonk ihm pries ehnt • hahl • tuhn*
What's this amount for?	**Wofür ist diese Summe?** *voh • fewr ihsht dee • zuh soo • muh*
I didn't have that. I had…	**Das hatte ich nicht. Ich hatte …** *dahs hah • tuh eekh neekht eekh hah • tuh …*
Can I…?	**Kann ich …?** *kahn eekh …*
pay with a credit card	**mit Kreditkarte bezahlen** *miht kreh • deet • kahr • tuh beht • sahl • uhn*
have a receipt	**eine Quittung haben** *ien • uh kvee • toonk hah • buhn*

have an itemized bill	**eine aufgeschlüsselte Rechnung haben**
	ien • uh owf • guh • shlew • sehl • tuh
	rehkh • oong • uhn hah • buhn
That was delicious!	**Das war lecker!**
	dahs vahr leh • khehr
I've already paid.	**Ich habe schon bezahlt.**
	eekh hah • buh shohn beht • sahlt

MEALS & COOKING

BREAKFAST

der Apfelsaft	apple juice
dehr ah • pfuhl • zahft	
der Aufschnitt	cold cuts
dehr owf • shniht	[charcuterie]
das Brot	bread
dahs broht	
das Brötchen	roll
dahs brert • khuhn	
die Butter	butter
dee boo • tehr	
das ... Ei	...egg
dahs ... ie	
hart/weich gekochte	hard-/soft-boiled
hahrt/viekh guh • kohkh • tuh	
der Joghurt	yogurt
dehr yoh • goort	
der Kaffee/Tee ...	coffee/tea...
dehr kah • feh/tee ...	
entkoffeiniert	decaf
ehnt • koh • feh • een • eert	

mit Milch	with milk
miht mihlkh	
mit Süßstoff	with artificial
miht <u>zews</u> • shtohf	sweetener
mit Zucker	with sugar
miht <u>tsoo</u> • khuhr	
schwarz	black
shvahrts	
der Käse	cheese
dehr <u>kay</u> • zuh	
der Kräutertee	herbal tea
dehr <u>krow</u> • tehr • tee	
die Marmelade	jam/jelly
dee mahr • muh • <u>lah</u> • duh	
die Milch	milk
dee mihlkh	
der Muffin	muffin
dehr <u>moo</u> • fihn	
das Müsli	granola [muesli]
dahs <u>mew</u> • slee	
das Omelett	omelet
dahs <u>ohm</u> • luht	

> (i)
>
> **Das Frühstück** (breakfast) can range from a large meal, usually served buffet style, to a simple dish of bread, jam and butter. **Das Mittagessen** (lunch), typically a large and heavy meal, is normally served from 12:00 to 2:00 p.m. In larger cities, many Germans will have lunch at a beer garden or hall with cafeteria-style service. **Das Abendessen** (dinner) is served from 6:00 to 9:00 p.m. and is usually a light meal.

der Orangensaft *dehr oh • rahng • uhn • zahft*	orange juice
der Pampelmusensaft *dehr pahm • puhl • moo • zuhn • zahft*	grapefruit juice
das Rührei *dahs rew • rie*	scrambled egg
der Saft *dehr zahft*	juice
der Schinken *dehr shihn • kuhn*	ham
das Spiegelei *dahs shpeeg • uh • lle*	fried egg
der Toast *dehr tohst*	toast
das Wasser *dahs vah • sehr*	water

APPETIZERS

die Appetithäppchen *dee ah • peh • teet • hehp • khehn*	finger sandwiches
die Aufschnittplatte *dee owf • shniht • plah • tuh*	cold cuts served with bread

der Bismarckhering	marinated herring
dehr bees • mahrk • heh • reeng	with onions
die Fleischpastete	meat pâté
dee fliesh • pah • steh • tuh	
die Gänseleberpastete	goose liver pâté
dee gehn • zehl • leh • behr • pah • steh • tuh	
die gefüllten Champignons	stuffed mushrooms
dee geh • fewl • tehn shahm • pee • nyohns	
der gemischte Salat	mixed salad
dehr geh • meesh • tuh sah • laht	
die Käseplatte	cheese platter
dee kay • zuh • plah • tuh	
das Knoblauchbrot	garlic bread
dahs knoh • blowkh • broht	
der Krabbencocktail	shrimp cocktail
dehr krahb • behn • kohk • tayl	
die russischen Eier	hard-boiled eggs
dee roo • see • shuh ier	with mayonnaise
der Räucherlachs	smoked salmon
dehr roy • khurt • lahks	
der Salat	salad
dehr sah • laht	
die Soleier	eggs boiled in brine
dee soh • lier	
der Tomatensalat	tomato salad
dehr toh • mah • tehn • sah • laht	
der Wurstsalat	cold cuts with onion
dehr voorst • sah • laht	and oil

SOUP

die Backerbsensuppe	broth with crisp,
dee bahk • ehrb • sehn • zoo • puh	round noodles
die Bohnensuppe	bean soup
dee boh • nuhn • zoo • puh	

die Champignoncremesuppe	cream of mushroom
dee <u>shahm</u> • pee • nyohn • krehm • zoo • puh	soup
die Erbsensuppe	pea soup
dee <u>ehrb</u> • zuhn • zoo • puh	
die Fleischbrühe	bouillon
dee <u>fliesh</u> • brew • uh	
die Frittatensuppe	broth with pancake
dee free • <u>tah</u> • tehn • zoo • puh	strips
die Frühlingssuppe	spring vegetable
dee <u>frew</u> • leeng • zoo • puh	soup
die Gemüsesuppe	vegetable soup
dee guh • <u>mew</u> • zuh • zoo • puh	
die Gulaschsuppe	stewed beef in a
dee <u>gool</u> • ahsh • zoo • puh	spicy soup
die Hühnersuppe	chicken soup
dee <u>hewn</u> • ehr • zoo • puh	
die klare Gemüsebrühe	vegetable broth
dee <u>klah</u> • ruh geh • <u>mew</u> • zuh • brew • uh	
die Linsensuppe	lentil soup
dee <u>leen</u> • zehn • zoo • puh	
die Semmelknödelsuppe	bread dumpling soup
dee <u>zeh</u> • mehl • kner • dehl • zoo • puh	
die Tomatensuppe	tomato soup
dee toh • <u>mah</u> • tuhn • zoo • puh	
die Zwiebelsuppe	onion soup
dee <u>tsvee</u> • behl • zoo • puh	

FISH & SEAFOOD

der Aal	eel
dehr ahl	
die Auster	oyster
dee <u>ow</u> • stehr	
die Brachse	bream
dee <u>brahk</u> • suh	

der Barsch	perch
dehr bahrsh	
der Brathering	fried sour herring
dehr brah • theh • reeng	
der Dorsch	cod
dehr dohrsh	
die Forelle	trout
dee foh • reh • luh	
die Garnele	shrimp
dee gahr • neh • luh	
der Heilbutt	halibut
dehr hiel • boot	
der Hering	herring
dehr heh • rihng	
der Hummer	lobster
dehr hoo • mehr	
der Krebs	crab
dehr krehbs	
der Lachs	salmon
dehr lahks	
die Makrele	mackerel
dee mah • kreh • luh	
die Muschel	clam
dee moo • shuhl	

der Oktopus	octopus
dehr <u>ohk</u> • toh • poos	
die Sardelle	anchovy
dee sahr • <u>deh</u> • luh	
die Sardine	sardine
dee zahr • <u>dee</u> • nuh	
die Scholle	flounder
dee <u>shoh</u> • luh	
der Schwertfisch	swordfish
dehr <u>shvehrt</u> • fihsh	
der Seebarsch	sea bass
dehr <u>zeh</u> • bahrsh	
die Seezunge	sole
dee <u>zeh</u> • tsoong • uh	
der Tintenfisch	squid
dehr <u>tihn</u> • tuhn • fihsh	
der Thunfisch	tuna
dehr <u>toon</u> • fihsh	

MEAT & POULTRY

die Berliner Buletten	fried meatballs,
dee behr • <u>lee</u> • nuh boo • <u>leh</u> • tehn	a specialty of Berlin
der Braten	roast
dehr <u>brah</u> • tuhn	
die Bratwurst	fried sausage
dee <u>braht</u> • voorst	
die Ente	duck
dee <u>ehn</u> • tuh	
das Filet	filet
dahs <u>fee</u> • leh	
der Fleischkäse	a kind of meatloaf
dehr <u>fliesh</u> • kay • zuh	
die Frikadelle	fried meatballs
dee free • kah • <u>dehl</u> • luh	

das Gulasch *dahs gool•ahsh*	stewed beef with spicy paprika gravy
der Hackbraten *dehr hahk•brah•tuhn*	meatloaf
das Hackfleisch *dahs hahk•fliesh*	ground meat
das Hühnchen *dahs hewn•khuhn*	chicken
das Spanferkel *dahs shpahn•fehr•kehl*	crunchy roasted suckling pig
das Kalbfleisch *dahs kahlb•fliesh*	veal
das Kaninchen *dahs kah•nihn•khehn*	rabbit
das Kotelett *dahs koht•leht*	pork chop
das Lamm *dahs lahm*	lamb
die Leber *dee leh•behr*	liver
die Niere *dee nee•ruh*	kidney
das Pökelfleisch *dahs pehr•kehl•fliesh*	pickled meat
der Rinderbraten *dehr reen•dehr•brah•tuhn*	roast beef
das Rindfleisch *dahs rihnt•fliesh*	beef
die Rouladen *dee roo•lah•dehn*	stuffed beef slices, rolled and braised in brown gravy
der Sauerbraten *dehr zow•ehr•brah•tuhn*	beef roast, marinated with herbs, in a rich sauce

der Schinken   ham
dehr shihn • kuhn

der Schinkenspeck   bacon
dehr shihn • kuhn • shpehk

das Schmorfleisch   stewed meat
dahs shmohr • fliesh

das Schweinefleisch   pork
dahs shvien • uh • fliesh

der Schweinebraten   roast pork
dehr shvien • brah • tuhn

das Steak   steak
dahs shtayhk

der Tafelspitz   Viennese-style boiled
dehr tah • fehl • shpeets   beef

der Truthahn   turkey
dehr troot • hahn

das Wiener Schnitzel   veal cutlet
dahs viee • nehr shniht • tzehl

die Wurst   sausage
dee voorst

die Zunge   tongue
dee tsoong • uh

VEGETABLES & STAPLES

die Artischocke   artichoke
dee ahr • tee • shoh • kuh

die Aubergine   eggplant [aubergine]
dee ow • behr • gee • neh

die Avocado   avocado
dee ah • voh • kah • doh

die Bohnen   beans
dee boh • nuhn

die grünen Bohnen   green beans
dee grew • nuhn boh • nuhn

der Blumenkohl	cauliflower
dehr bloo • muhn • kohl	
der Brokkoli	broccoli
dehr broh • koh • lee	
die Erbse	pea
dee ehrb • zuh	
das gemischte Gemüse	mixed vegetables
dahs geh • meesh • tuh geh • mew • zuh	
das Gemüse	vegetable
dahs geh • mew • zuh	
die Gurke	cucumber
dee goor • kuh	
die Kartoffel	potato
dee kahr • toh • fuhl	
der Kartoffelbrei	mashed potato
dehr kahr • toh • fehl • brie	
der Knoblauch	garlic
dehr knoh • blowkh	
der Kohl	cabbage
dehr kohl	
der Krautsalat	coleslaw
dehr krowt • sah • laht	
der Mais	corn
dehr mies	
der Maiskolben	corn on the cob
dehr mies • kohl • behn	
die Möhre	carrot
dee mer • ruh	
die Olive	olive
dee oh • lee • vuh	
der rote/grüne Paprika	red/green pepper
dehr roh • teh/ grew • neh pah • pree • kuh	
die Pasta	pasta
dee pah • stah	

die Pellkartoffeln	boiled, unpeeled
dee pehl • kahr • toh • fehl • ehn	potatoes
der Pilz	mushroom
dehr pihlts	
der Reis	rice
dehr ries	
der Rettich	radish
dehr reh • teekh	
das Roggenbrot	rye bread
dahs roh • gehn • broht	
der Salat	lettuce
dehr sah • laht	
der Spargel	asparagus
dehr shpahr • gehl	
der Spinat	spinach
dehr shpee • naht	
die Tomate	tomato
dee toh • mah • teh	
die Zucchini	zucchini [courgette]
dee tsoo • khee • nee	
die Zwiebel	onion
dee tsvee • buhl	

FRUIT

die Ananas	pineapple
dee ah • nah • nahs	
der Apfel	apple
dehr ahp • fuhl	
die Apfelsine	orange
dee ah • pfehl • zee • nuh	
die Banane	banana
dee bah • nah • nuh	
die Birne	pear
dee beer • nuh	

die Blaubeere	blueberry
dee <u>blow</u> • beh • ruh	
die Erdbeere	strawberry
dee <u>ehrd</u> • beh • ruh	
die Himbeere	raspberry
dee <u>hihm</u> • beh • ruh	
die Kirsche	cherry
dee <u>keer</u> • shuh	
die Limette	lime
dee lee • <u>meh</u> • tuh	
die Melone	melon
dee meh • <u>loh</u> • nuh	
das Obst	fruit
dahs ohpst	
die Pampelmuse	grapefruit
dee <u>pahm</u> • pehl • moo • zuh	
der Pfirsich	peach
dehr <u>pfeer</u> • zeekh	
die Pflaume	plum
dee <u>pflow</u> • muh	
die rote/schwarze Johannisbeere	red/black currant
dee <u>roh</u> • tuh/	
<u>shvahr</u> • tsuh yoh • <u>hah</u> • nihs • beh • ruh	

die Weintraube   grape
dee vien • trow • buh
die Zitrone   lemon
dee tsee • troh • nuh

CHEESE

der Appenzeller   hard cheese from
dehr ah • pehn • tseh • lehr   Switzerland
der Blauschimmelkäse   blue cheese

dehr blow • shihm • mehl • kay • zuh
der Emmentaler   mild Swiss cheese
dehr ehm • mehn • tah • lehr
der Frischkäse   cream cheese
dehr freesh • kay • zuh
der Handkäse   sharp, soft cheese
dehr hahnt • kay • zuh
die Käseplatte   cheese platte
dee kay • zuh • plah • tuhr
der Schafskäse   feta cheese
dehr shahf • kay • zuh
der Tilsiter   semi-soft Austrian
dehr teel • seet • ehr   cheese
der Ziegenkäse   goat cheese
dehr tsee • guhn • kay • zuh

DESSERT

der Apfelkuchen   apple pie or tart
dehr ah • pfuhl • kookh • uhn
das Eis   ice cream
dahs ies
der Käsekuchen   cheesecake
dehr kay • zuh • kookh • uhn

der Krapfen	fritter
dehr krah • pfehn	
die Makrone	macaroon
dee mah • kroh • nuh	
das Marzipan	marzipan
dahs mahr • tsee • pahn	
der Obstsalat	fruit salad
dehr ohpst • sah • laht	
die Rote Grütze	berry pudding
dee roh • tuh grewt • zuh	
die Schwarzwälder Kirschtorte	Black Forest
dee schvahrts • vahl • dehr	chocolate cake with
keersh • tohr • tuh	cherries
die Torte	cake
dee tohr • tuh	

SAUCES & CONDIMENTS

salt	**salz**
sahlts	
pepper	**pfeffer**
pfehf • fehr	
mustard	**senf**
sehnf	
ketchup	**ketchup**
ket • shahp	

AT THE MARKET

Where are the trolleys/baskets?	**Wo sind die Einkaufswagen/ Einkaufskörbe?**
	voh zihnt dee ien • kowfs • vah • guhn/ ien • kowfs • kehr • buh
Where is…?	**Wo ist …?**
	voh ihsht …

I'd like some of that/this.	**Ich möchte etwas von dem/diesem.**
	eekh merkh • tuh eht • vahs fohn dehm/dee • zuhm
Can I taste it?	**Kann ich es kosten?**
	kahn eekh ehs kohs • tuhn
I'd like…	**Ich möchte …**
	eekh merkh • tuh …
a kilo/	**ein Kilo/halbes Kilo …**
half-kilo of…	*ien kee • loh/hahl • buhs kee • loh …*
a liter of…	**einen Liter …**
	ien • uhn lee • tehr …
a piece of…	**ein Stück …**
	ien shtewk …
a slice of…	**eine Scheibe …**
	ien • uh shie • buh …
More/less	**Mehr/Weniger**
	mehr/veh • nee • guhr
How much?	**Wie viel kostet das?**
	vee feel kohs • tuht dahs
Where do I pay?	**Wo bezahle ich?**
	voh beht • sahl • uh eekh
A bag, please.	**Eine Tüte, bitte.**
	ien • uh tew • tuh biht • tuh

I'm being helped. **Ich werde schon bedient.**
eekh <u>vehr</u> • duh shohn buh • <u>deent</u>

For Meals & Cooking, see page 175.

YOU MAY HEAR...

Kann ich Ihnen helfen?
kahn eekh <u>eehn</u> • uhn <u>hehl</u> • fuhn

Can I help you?

Was möchten Sie?
vahs <u>merkh</u> • tuhn zee

What would you like?

Noch etwas?
nohkh <u>eht</u> • vahs

Anything else?

Das macht ... Euro.
dahs mahkht ... <u>oy</u> • roh

That's...euros.

Local markets that sell fresh produce and homemade goods can be found in most cities throughout Germany. The days and hours of operation vary widely. Your hotel concierge or a tourist information office can provide details.

IN THE KITCHEN

bottle opener	**der Flaschenöffner**
	dehr <u>flah</u> • shuhn • erf • nehr
bowl	**die Schüssel**
	dee <u>shew</u> • suhl
can opener	**der Dosenöffner**
	dehr <u>doh</u> • zuhn • erf • nuhr

corkscrew	**der Korkenzieher**
	dehr kohr • kuhn • tsee • uhr
cup	**die Tasse**
	dee tah • suh
fork	**die Gabel**
	dee gah • buhl
frying pan	**die Bratpfanne**
	dee braht • pfah • nuh
glass	**das Glas**
	dahs glahs
(steak) knife	**das (Steak-) Messer**
	dahs (shtehk •) meh • sehr
measuring cup	**der Messbecher**
	dehr mehs • beh • khuhr
measuring spoon	**der Messlöffel**
	dehr mehs • ler • fuhl
napkin	**die Serviette**
	dee sehr • vyeh • tuh
plate	**der Teller**
	dehr teh • lehr
pot	**der Topf**
	dehr tohpf
spatula	**der Spatel**
	dehr shpah • tuhl
spoon	**der Löffel**
	dehr ler • fuhl

Measurements in Europe are metric – and that applies to the weight of food too. If you tend to think in pounds and ounces, it's worth brushing up on what the metric equivalent is before you go shopping for fruit and veg in markets and supermarkets. Five hundred grams, or half a kilo, is a common quantity to order, and that converts to just over a pound (17.65 ounces, to be precise).

DRINKS

NEED TO KNOW

The wine list/drink menu, please.	**Die Weinkarte/Getränkekarte, bitte.** *dee vien • kahr • tuh/ geh • trehnk • uh • kahr • tuh biht • tuh*
What do you recommend?	**Was empfehlen Sie?** *vahs ehm • pfeh • luhn zee*
I'd like a bottle/ glass of red/ white wine.	**Ich möchte gern eine Flasche/ein Glas Rotwein/Weißwein.** *eekh merkh • tuh gehrn ien • uh flah • shuh/ien glahs roht • vien/ vies • vien*
The house wine, please.	**Den Hauswein, bitte.** *dehn hows • vien biht • tuh*
Another bottle/glass, please.	**Noch eine Flasche/ein Glas, bitte.** *nohkh ien • uh flah • shuh/ien glahs biht • tuh*
I'd like a local beer.	**Ich möchte gern ein Bier aus der Region.** *eekh merkh • tuh gehrn ien beer ows dehr rehg • yohn*

Can I buy you a drink?	**Darf ich Ihnen einen ausgeben?**
	dahrf eekh <u>eehn</u> • uhn <u>ows</u> • geh • buhn
Cheers!	**Prost!**
	prohst
A coffee/tea, please.	**Einen Kaffee/Tee, bitte.**
	<u>ien</u> • uhn kah • <u>feh</u>/tee <u>biht</u> • tuh
Black.	**Schwarz.**
	shvahrts
With...	**Mit ...**
	miht ...
milk	**Milch**
	mihlkh
sugar	**Zucker**
	<u>tsoo</u> • kehr
artificial sweetener	**Süßstoff**
	<u>zews</u> • shtohf
..., please.	**..., bitte.**
	... <u>biht</u> • tuh
A juice	**Einen Saft**
	<u>ien</u> • uhn zahft
A soda	**Eine Cola**
	<u>ien</u> • uh <u>koh</u> • lah
A still/sparkling water	**Ein stilles Wasser/Wasser mit Kohlensäure**
	ien <u>shtihl</u> • uhs <u>vah</u> • sehr/<u>vah</u> • sehr miht <u>kohl</u> • ehn • zoy • ruh

NON-ALCOHOLIC DRINKS

die Cola
dee <u>koh</u> • lah   soda

(i)

Kaffee (coffee) is popular in Germany and a fresh
cup can be found at a **Café** or **Kaffeehaus**. **Kräutertee**
(herbal tea) is another common beverage, and pharmacies,
supermarkets and health-food stores carry a variety of teas.

der Kaffee
dehr kah • feh   coffee
der Kakao
dehr kah • kah • ow   hot chocolate
die Milch
dee mihlkh   milk
der Saft
dehr zahft   juice
der (Eis-)Tee
dehr (ies) tee   (iced) tea
das stille Wasser/Wasser mit
Kohlensäure   still/sparkling water
dahs shtihl • uh vah • sehr/vah • sehr miht
kohl • ehn • zoy • ruh

YOU MAY HEAR...

(speech icon)

Möchten Sie etwas trinken?   Can I get you
merkh • tuhn zee eht • vahs trihn • kuhn   a drink?
Mit Milch oder Zucker?   With milk or
miht mihlkh oh • dehr tsoo • kehr   sugar?
Stilles Wasser oder mit Kohlensäure?   Still or sparkling
shtihl • uhs vah • sehr oh • dehr miht   water?
koh • lehn • zoy • ruh

APERITIFS, COCKTAILS & LIQUEURS

der Gin   gin
dehr djihn
der Rum   rum
dehr room
der Scotch   scotch
dehr skohch
der Tequila   tequila
dehr teh • kee • lah
der Weinbrand   brandy
dehr vien • brahnt
der Whisky   whisky
dehr vees • kee
der Wodka   vodka
dehr voht • kah

BEER

as Flaschenbier   bottled beer
dahs flah • shuhn • beer
das Bier vom Fass   draft beer
dahs beer fohm fahs

ⓘ

There are more than 1,000 breweries in Germany, producing more than 5,000 different brands of beer. Styles include: **Altbier** (high hops content, similar to British ale), **Bockbier** (high malt content), **Hefeweizen** (pale, made from wheat), **Kölsch** (lager, brewed in Cologne), **Malzbier** (dark and sweet) and **Pilsener** (pale and strong). Popular German brands include: **Augustiner™**, **Beck's™**, **Jever™**, **Löwenbräu™** and **Spaten™**.

das Helle/Pilsner dahs <u>heh</u> • luh/pihls • nehr	lager/pilsner
die Halbe dee <u>hahlb</u> • uh	pint
das … Bier dahs … beer	…beer
dunkle/helle <u>doon</u> • kluh/<u>heh</u> • luh	dark/light
regionale/importierte reh • gyoh • <u>nah</u> • luh/ eem • pohr • <u>teer</u> • tuh	local/imported
alkoholfreie ahl • koh • hohl • <u>frie</u> • uh	non-alcoholic

WINE

der Champagner dehr shahm • <u>pahn</u> • yehr	champagne
der Wein dehr vien	wine
der Dessertwein dehr deh • <u>sehrt</u> • vien	dessert wine
der Hauswein/Tischwein	house/table wine

dehr <u>hows</u> • vien/<u>tihsh</u> • vien

der Rotwein/Weißwein — red/white wine
dehr <u>roht</u> • vien/<u>vies</u> • vien

der trockene/liebliche Wein — dry/sweet wine
dehr <u>troh</u> • keh • neh/<u>lee</u> • blee • kheh vien

der Schaumwein — sparkling wine
dehr <u>showm</u> • vien

ON THE MENU

der Aal *dehr ahl*	eel
die Ananas *dee <u>ahn</u> • ah • nahs*	pineapple
der Aperitif *dehr ah • pehr • ee • <u>teef</u>*	aperitif
der Apfel *dehr <u>ahp</u> • fehl*	apple
die Apfelsine *dee ah • pfuhl • <u>zee</u> • nuh*	orange
der Apfelwein *dehr <u>ah</u> • pfuhl • vien*	cider (alcoholic)
die Aprikose *dee ah • pree • <u>koh</u> • zuh*	apricot
die Artischocke *dee ahr • tee • <u>shoh</u> • kuh*	artichoke
die Aubergine *dee <u>ow</u> • behr • gee • nuh*	eggplant [aubergine]
der Aufschnitt *dehr <u>owf</u> • shniht*	cold cuts [charcuterie]
die Auster *dee <u>ows</u> • tuhr*	oyster
die Avocado *dee ah • voh • <u>kah</u> • doh*	avocado

die Backpflaume *dee <u>bahk</u> • pflow • muh*	prune
der Bacon *dehr <u>bah</u> • kohn*	bacon
die Banane *dee bah • <u>nah</u> • nuh*	banana
der Barsch *dehr bahrsh*	bass
das Basilikum *dahs hah • <u>zee</u> • lee • koom*	basil
das Bier *dahs beer*	beer
die Birne *dee <u>beer</u> • nuh*	pear
die Blaubeere *dee <u>blow</u> • beh • ruh*	blueberry
der Blauschimmelkäse *dehr <u>blow</u> • shihm • mehl • kay • zuh*	blue cheese
der Blumenkohl *dehr <u>bloo</u> • muhn • kohl*	cauliflower
die Blutwurst *dee <u>bloot</u> • voorst*	blood sausage
die Bohne *dee <u>boh</u> • nuh*	bean

die Bouillon	broth
dee boo•yohn	
der Branntwein	brandy
dehr brahnt•vien	
der Braten	roast
dehr brah•tuhn	
die Brombeere	blackberry
dee brohm•beh•ruh	
das Brot	bread
dahs broht	
das Brötchen	roll
dahs brert•khehn	
die Brunnenkresse	watercress
dee broo•nuhn•kreh•zuh	
die (Hühnchen-) Brust	breast (of chicken)
dee (hewn•khehn-) broost	
die Butter	butter
dee boo•tehr	
die Buttermilch	buttermilk
dee boo•tehr•mihlkh	
die Cashewnuss	cashew
dee keh•shoo•noos	
der Chikorée	chicory
dehr chee•koh•reh	
die Chilischote	chili pepper
dee chee•lee•shoh•tuh	
die Cola	soda
dee koh•lah	
der Cracker	cracker
dehr kreh•kehr	
die Datteln	dates
dee dah•tuhln	
der Dessertwein	dessert wine
dehr deh•zehrt•vien	

der Dill
dehr dihl

dill

der Donut
dehr doh•nuht

doughnut

der Dorsch
dehr dohrsh

cod

das Ei
dahs ie

egg

das Eigelb
dahs ie•gehlb

egg yolk

der Eierkuchen
dehr ier•koo•khuhn

pancake

das Eis
dahs ies

ice cream

der Eiswürfel
dehr ies•vewr•fehl

ice (cube)

das Eiweiß
dahs ie•vies

egg white

die Endivie
dee ehn•dee•vee•uh

endive

die Ente
dee ehn•tuh

duck

die Erbsen
dee ehrb•zuhn

peas

die Erdbeere
dee ehrd•beh•ruh

strawberry

die Erdnuss
dee ehrd•noos

peanut

der Essig
dehr eh•zeek

vinegar

das Estragon
dahs eh•strah•gohn

tarragon

der Fasan
dehr fah•zahn

pheasant

die Feige	fig
dee <u>fie</u> • guh	
der Fenchel	fennel
dehr <u>fehn</u> • khehl	
der Fisch	fish
dehr fihsh	
das Fleisch	meat
dahs fliesh	
die Fleischstücke	chopped meat
dee <u>fliesh</u> • shtew • kuh	
die Forelle	trout
dee foh • <u>reh</u> • luh	
die Gans	goose
dee gahns	
die Gänseleberpastete	goose liver pâté
dee <u>gehn</u> • zehl • leh • behr • pah • steh • tuh	
die Garnele	shrimp
dee gahr • <u>neh</u> • luh	
das Gebäck	pastry
dahs guh • <u>behk</u>	
das Geflügel	poultry
dahs guh • <u>flew</u> • gehl	
das Gemüse	vegetable
dahs geh • <u>mew</u> • zuh	

die Gewürze
dee guh • vewr • tsuh

spices

die Gewürzgurke
dee guh • vewrts • goor • kuh

pickle/gherkin

der Gin
dehr djihn

gin

der Granatapfel
dehr grah • naht • ahp • fehl

pomegranate

die grünen Bohnen
dee grew • nuhn boh • nuhn

green beans

die Guave
dee gwah • veh

guava

die Gurke
dee goor • kuh

cucumber

die Hachse
dee hahk • suh

shank

der Hamburger
dehr hahm • boor • gehr

hamburger

der Hammel
dehr hah • mehl

mutton

die Haselnuss
dee hah • zuhl • noos

hazelnut

der Heilbutt
dehr hiel • boot

halibut

die Henne
dee heh • nuh

hen

der Hering
dehr heh • reeng

herring

das Herz
dahs hehrts

heart

die Himbeere
dee heem • beh • ruh

raspberry

der Honig
dehr hoh • neek

honey

der Hotdog *dehr hoht • dohg*	hot dog
das Hühnchen *dahs hewn • khehn*	chicken
der Hummer *dehr hoo • mehr*	lobster
der Hüttenkäse *dehr hew • tuhn • kay • zuh*	cottage cheese
der Imbiss *dehr ihm • buhs*	snack
der Ingwer *dehr eeng • vehr*	ginger
die Innereien *dee ihn • eh • rie • uhn*	organ meat [offal]
der Joghurt *dehr yoh • goort*	yogurt
der Kaffee *dehr kah • feh*	coffee
das Kalb *dahs kahlb*	veal
das Kaninchen *dahs kah • neen • khehn*	rabbit
die Kaper *dee kah • pehr*	caper
das Karamell *dahs kah • rah • mehl*	caramel
die Kartoffel *dee kahr • toh • fehl*	potato
die Kartoffelchips *dee kahr • toh • fehl • cheeps*	potato chips [crisps]
der Käse *dehr kay • zuh*	cheese
die Kastanie *dee kah • stahn • yuh*	chestnut

der Keks
dehr keks

cookie [biscuit]

der Kerbel
dehr kehr•behl

chervil

der Ketchup
dehr keh•chuhp

ketchup

die Kichererbse
dee kee•khehr•ehrb•zuh

chickpea

die Kirsche
dee keer•shuh

cherry

die Kiwi
dee kee•vee

kiwi

der Kloß
dehr klohs

dumpling

der Knoblauch
dehr knoh•blowkh

garlic

die Koblauchsauce
dee knoh•blowkh•zow•suh

garlic sauce

der Kohl
dehr kohl

cabbage

die Kokosnuss
dee koh•kohs•noos

coconut

das Kompott
dahs kohm•poht

stewed fruit

die Konfitüre
dee kohn•fee•tew•ruh

jelly

der Koriander
dehr koh•ree•ahn•dehr

cilantro [coriander]

die Kräuter
dee kroyt•uhr

herbs

die Kraftbrühe
dee krahft•brew•uh

consommé

der Krebs
dehr krehbs

crab

das Krustentier
dahs kroos • tehn • tyehr
shellfish

der Kuchen
dehr kookh • uhn
pie

der Kümmel
dehr kew • mehl
caraway

der Kürbis
dehr kewr • bees
squash

die Kutteln
dee koo • tehln
tripe

der Lachs
dehr lahks
salmon

das Lamm
dahs lahm
lamb

die Lauchzwiebel
dee lowkh • svee • buhl
scallion [spring onion]

die Leber
dee leh • buhr
liver

die Lende
dee lehn • duh
loin

das Lendenfilet
dahs lehn • dehn • fee • leh
sirloin

der Likör
dehr lee • ker
liqueur

die Limette
dee lee • meh • tuh
lime

die Limonade
dee lee • moh • nah • duh
lemonade

die Linse
dee leen • zuh
lentil

das Loorbeerblatt
dahs lohr • behr • blaht
bay leaf

der Mais
dehr mies
sweet corn

das Maismehl *dahs <u>mies</u> • mehl*	cornmeal
die Makkaroni *dee mah • kah • <u>roh</u> • nee*	macaroni
die Makrele *dee mah • <u>krehl</u> • uh*	mackerel
die Mandarine *dee mahn • dah • <u>reen</u> • uh*	tangerine
die Mandel *dee <u>mahn</u> • duhl*	almond
die Mango *dee <u>mahn</u> • goh*	mango
die Margarine *dee mahr • guh • <u>ree</u> • nuh*	margarine
die Marmelade *dee mahr • muh • <u>lah</u> • duh*	marmalade/jam
das Marzipan *dahs <u>mahr</u> • tsee • pahn*	marzipan
die Mayonnaise *dee mah • yoh • <u>nay</u> • zuh*	mayonnaise
die Meerbarbe *dee <u>mehr</u> • bahr • buh*	red mullet
die Meeresfrüchte *dee <u>mch</u> • rehs • frewkh • tuh*	seafood

die Melone
dee meh • loh • nuh

melon

die Milch
dee mihlkh

milk

das Milchmixgetränk
dahs mihlkh • mihks • geh • traynk

milk shake

die Minze
dee mihn • tsuh

mint

die Möhre
dee mer • ruh

carrot

die Muschel
dee moo • shehl

clam

der Muskat
dehr moos • kaht

nutmeg

die Nelke
dee nehl • kuh

clove

die Niere
dee nee • ruh

kidney

die Nudel
dee noo • dehl

noodle

der Nugat
dehr noo • gaht

nougat

die Nüsse
dee new • suh

nuts

das Obst
dahs ohbst

fruit

der Ochse
dehr ohkh • suh

ox

der Ochsenschwanz
dehr ohk • sehn • shvahnts

oxtail

der Oktopus
dehr ohk • toh • poos

octopus

die Olive
dee oh • lee • veh

olive

das Olivenöl olive oil
dahs oh • lee • vehn • erl

das Omelett omelet
dahs ohm • leht

der Orangenlikör orange liqueur
dehr oh • rahn • jehn • lee • ker

das Oregano oregano
dahs oh • reh • gah • noh

die Pampelmuse grapefruit
dee pahm • puhl • moo • zuh

der Pansen tripe
dehr pahn • sehn

die Papaya papaya
dee pah • pah • yah

der Paprika paprika
dehr pah • pree • kuh

die Paprikaschote pepper (vegetable)
dee pah • pree • kah • shoh • tuh

die Pastinake parsnip
dee pah • stec • nahk • uh

die Pekannuss pecan
dee pch • kahn • noos

das Perlhuhn guinea fowl
dahs pehrl • hoon

die Petersilie parsley
dee peh • tehr • see • lee • uh

der Pfannkuchen pancake
dehr pfahn • koo • khuhn

der Pfeffer pepper (seasoning)
dehr pfeh • fehr

der Pfirsich peach
dehr pfeer • zeekh

die Pflaume plum
dee pflow • muh

der Pilz *dehr pihlts*	mushroom
die Pizza *dee pee•tsah*	pizza
die Pommes frites *dee pohm freets*	French fries
der Porree *dehr poh•reh*	leek
der Portwein *dehr pohrt•vien*	port
die Preiselbeere *dee prie•zuhl•beh•ruh*	cranberry
der Rahmkäse *dehr rahm•kay•zuh*	cream cheese
der Reis *dehr ries*	rice
der Rettich *dehr reh•teekh*	radish
der Rhabarber *dehr rah•bahr•behr*	rhubarb
der Rinderbraten *dehr reen•dehr•brah•tuhn*	roast beef
das Rindfleisch *dahs rihnt•fliesh*	beef

der Rosenkohl
dehr roh•zuhn•kohl
Brussels sprouts

die Rosine
dee roh•zee•nuh
raisin

der Rosmarin
dehr rohs•mah•reen
rosemary

die rote Johannisbeere
dee roh•tuh yoh•hah•nihs•beh•ruh
red currant

der Rotkohl
dehr rohl•kohl
red cabbage

die Rübe
dee rew•beh
beet/turnip

der Rum
dehr room
rum

der Safran
dehr zahf•rahn
saffron

der Saft
dehr zahft
juice

die Sahne
dee zah•nuh
cream

die Salami
dee zah•lah•mee
salami

der Salat
dehr sah•laht
lettuce/salad

der Salbei
dehr zahl•bie
sage

das Salz
dahs zahlts
salt

das Sandwich
dahs sahnd•weetsh
sandwich

die Sardelle
dee sahr•dehl•uh
anchovy

die Sardine
dee zahr•dee•nuh
sardine

die Sauce
dee zows • uh

sauce

die Sauerkirsche
dee zow • ehr • keer • shuh

sour cherry

die saure Sahne
dee zow • ruh zah • nuh

sour cream

die Schalotte
dee shah • loh • tuh

shallot

die scharfe Pfeffersauce
dee shahr • fuh pfeh • fehr • zow • suh

hot pepper sauce

das Schaumgebäck
dahs showm • guh • behk

meringue

der Schellfisch
dehr shehl • fihsh

haddock

der Schinken
dehr sheen • kuhn

ham

die Schlagsahne
dee shlahg • zah • nuh

whipped cream

die Schnecke
dee shnehkh • uh

snail

der Schnittlauch
dehr shniht • lowkh

chives

das Schnitzel
dahs shniht • tzuhl

chop

die Schokolade
dee shoh • koh • lah • duh

chocolate

die Schulter
dee shool • tehr

shoulder

die schwarze Johannisbeere
dee shvahr • tsuh yoh • hah • nees • beh • ruh

black currant

das Schweinefleisch
dahs shvien • uh • fliesh

pork

der Schwertfisch
dehr shvehrt • fihsh

swordfish

der Scotch *dehr skohtsh*	scotch
der Seebarsch *dehr <u>zeh</u> • bahrsh*	sea bass
der Seehecht *dehr <u>zeh</u> • hehkht*	hake
der Seeteufel *dehr <u>zeh</u> • toy • fuhl*	monkfish
die Seezunge *dee <u>zeh</u> • tsoong • uh*	sole
der Sellerie *dehr <u>zeh</u> • luh • ree*	celery
der Senf *dehr zehnf*	mustard
der Sherry *dehr <u>shehr</u> • ee*	sherry
der Sirup *dehr <u>zew</u> • roop*	syrup
das Soda-Wasser *dahs <u>soh</u> • dah-<u>vah</u> • sehr*	soda water
die Sojabohne *dee <u>zoh</u> • yah • boh • nuh*	soybean [soya bean]
die Sojamilch *dee <u>zoh</u> • yah • mihlkh*	soymilk [soya milk]

die Sojasauce *dee <u>zoh</u> • yah • zow • suh*	soy sauce
die Sojasprossen *dee <u>soh</u> • jah • shproh • suhn*	bean sprouts
die Spaghetti *dee shpah • <u>geh</u> • tee*	spaghetti
das Spanferkel *dahs <u>shpahn</u> • fehr • kehl*	crunchy roasted suckling pig
der Spargel *dehr <u>shpahr</u> • gehl*	asparagus
der Spinat *dehr shpee • <u>naht</u>*	spinach
die Spirituosen *dee shpee • ree • <u>twoh</u> • zuhn*	spirits
die Stachelbeere *dee <u>shtah</u> • khehl • beh • ruh*	gooseberry
das Steak *dahs stehk*	steak
die Suppe *dee <u>zoo</u> • puh*	soup
die Süßigkeiten *dee <u>zew</u> • seekh • kie • tuhn*	candy [sweets]
die Süßkartoffel *dee <u>zews</u> • kahr • toh • fuhl*	sweet potato

die süßsaure Sauce
dee zews•zow•ruh zow•suh
sweet and sour sauce

der Süßstoff
dehr zews•shtohf
sweetener

der Tee
dehr teh
tea

der Thunfisch
dehr toon•fihsh
tuna

der Thymian
dehr tew•mee•ahn
thyme

der Tintenfisch
dehr teen•tuhn•fihsh
squid

der Toast
dehr tohst
toast

das Tofu
dahs toh•foo
tofu

die Tomate
dee toh•mah•tuh
tomato

das Tonic
dahs toh•neek
tonic water

die Trüffel
dee trew•fuhl
truffles

der Truthahn
dehr troot•hahn
turkey

die Vanille
dee vah•nee•luh
vanilla

die Wachtel
dee vahkh•tehl
quail

die Waffel
dee vah•fuhl
waffle

die Walnuss
dee vahl•noos
walnut

das Wasser
dahs vah•sehr
water

die Wassermelone *dee vah • sehr • meh • loh • nuh*	watermelon
der Wein *dehr vien*	wine
die Weintrauben *dee vien • trow • buhn*	grapes
der Weizen *dehr vie • tsuhn*	wheat
der Wermut *dehr vehr • moot*	vermouth
der Whisky *dehr vees • kee*	whisky
das Wild *dahs vihlt*	game/venison
der Wodka *dehr vohd • kah*	vodka
die Wurst *dee voorst*	sausage
der Zackenbarsch *dehr tsah • kehn • bahrsh*	sea perch
das Zicklein *dahs tsihk • lien*	kid (young goat)
die Ziege *dee tsee • guh*	goat

der Ziegenkäse	goat cheese
dehr tsee • guhn • kay • zuh	
der Zimt	cinnamon
dehr tsihmt	
die Zitrone	lemon
dee tsee • troh • nuh	
die Zucchini	zucchini [courgette]
dee tsoo • kee • nee	
der Zucker	sugar
dehr tsoo • kehr	
die Zunge	tongue
dee tsoong • uh	
die Zwiebel	onion
dce tsvce • buhl	

GOING OUT

GOING OUT

NEED TO KNOW

What's there to do at night?	**Was kann man dort abends unternehmen?** *vahs kahn mahn dohrt ahb • uhnds oon • tehr • nehm • uhn*
Do you have a program of events?	**Haben Sie ein Veranstaltungsprogramm?** *hah • buhn zee ien fehr • ahn • shtahlt • oongs • prohg • rahm*
What's playing tonight?	**Was wird heute Abend aufgeführt?** *vahs vihrd hoyt • uh ahb • uhnd owf • guh • fewrt*
Where's...?	**Wo ist ...?** *voh ihst ...*
the downtown area	**das Stadtzentrum** *dahs shtadt • tsehn • troom*
the bar	**die Bar** *dee bahr*

the dance club	**der Tanzclub**
	dee <u>tahnts</u> • kloop
Is there a cover charge?	**Kostet es Eintritt?**
	<u>kohs</u> • tuht ehs <u>ien</u> • triht

ENTERTAINMENT

Can you recommend...?	**Können Sie ... empfehlen?**
	<u>kern</u> • uhn zee ... ehm • <u>pfeh</u> • luhn
a concert	**ein Konzert**
	ien kohn • <u>tsehrt</u>
a movie	**einen Film**
	<u>ien</u> • uhn feelm
an opera	**eine Oper**
	<u>ien</u> • uhn <u>oh</u> • pehr
a play	**ein Theaterstück**
	ien teh • <u>ah</u> • tehr • shtewk
When does it start/end?	**Wann beginnt/endet es?**
	vahn beh • <u>gihnt</u>/<u>ehnd</u> • eht ehs
Where's...?	**Wo ist ...?**
	voh ihst ...
the concert hall	**die Konzerthalle**
	dee kohn • <u>tsehrt</u> • hah • luh
the opera house	**das Opernhaus**
	dahs <u>oh</u> • pehrn • hows
the theater	**das Theater**
	dahs teh • <u>ah</u> • tehr
the arcade	**die Spielhalle?**
	dee shpeel • hah • luh
What's the dress code?	**Wie ist die Kleiderordnung?**
	vee ihst dee <u>klied</u> • ehr • ohrd • noong
I like...	**Mir gefällt ...**
	meer guh • <u>fehlt</u> ...

Bitte schalten Sie Ihre Handys aus.
_biht • tuh shahlt • uhn zee eehr • uh
hehnd • ees ows_

Turn off
your mobile
[cell] phones,
please.

(i)

---

classical music	**klassische Musik**
	klahs • ihsh • uh moo • zeek
folk music	**Volksmusik**
	fohlks • moo • zeek
jazz	**Jazz**
	djehz
pop music	**Popmusik**
	pohp • moo • zeek
rap	**Rap**
	rehp

For Tickets, see page 47.

NIGHTLIFE

What's there to do at night?	**Was kann man dort abends unternehmen?**
	vahs kahn mahn dohrt ahb • uhnds oont • ehr • nehm • uhn
Can you recommend...?	**Können Sie ... empfehlen?**
	kern • uhn zee ... ehm • pfeh • luhn
a bar	**eine Bar**
	ien • uh bahr
a cabaret	**eine Kabarettvorstellung**
	ie • nuh kah • bah • reht • fohr • shteh • loong
a casino	**ein Casino**
	ien kah • see • noh

a dance club	**einen Tanzclub**
	ien • uhn tahnts • kloop
a gay club	**einen Schwulenclub**
	ien • uhn shvoo • luhn • kloop
a jazz club	**einen Jazzclub**
	ien • uhn yahts • kloop
a club with German music	**ein Club mit deutscher Musik**
	ien cloob meet doyt • shuhr muh • seek
Is there live music?	**Gibt es dort Livemusik?**
	gihpt ehs dohrt llev • moo • zeek
How do I get there?	**Wie komme ich dorthin?**
	vee kohm • uh eekh dohrt • hihn
Is there a cover charge?	**Kostet es Eintritt?**
	kohs • tuht ehs ien • triht
Let's go dancing.	**Lass uns tanzen gehen.**
	ahs oons tahnt • suhn geh • uhn
Is this area safe at night?	**Ist dieses Gebiet bei Nacht sicher?**
	ihst dee • zuhs geh • beet bie nahkht zeek • hehr

ROMANCE

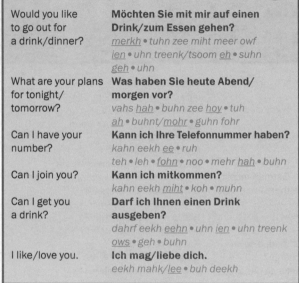

NEED TO KNOW

Would you like to go out for a drink/dinner?	**Möchten Sie mit mir auf einen Drink/zum Essen gehen?** _merkh • tuhn zee miht meer owf ien • uhn treenk/tsoom eh • suhn geh • uhn_
What are your plans for tonight/tomorrow?	**Was haben Sie heute Abend/ morgen vor?** _vahs hah • buhn zee hoy • tuh ah • buhnt/mohr • guhn fohr_
Can I have your number?	**Kann ich Ihre Telefonnummer haben?** _kahn eekh ee • ruh teh • leh • fohn • noo • mehr hah • buhn_
Can I join you?	**Kann ich mitkommen?** _kahn eekh miht • koh • muhn_
Can I get you a drink?	**Darf ich Ihnen einen Drink ausgeben?** _dahrf eekh eehn • uhn ien • uhn treenk ows • geh • buhn_
I like/love you.	**Ich mag/liebe dich.** _eekh mahk/lee • buh deekh_

THE DATING GAME

Would you like to go out... for coffee?	**Möchten Sie mit mir Kaffee trinken gehen?** _mehrkh • tuhn zee miht meer ien • uhn kah • feh trihnk • uhn geh • uhn_

Would you like to go out for a drink?	**Möchten Sie mit mir etwas trinken gehen?**
	merkht • uhn zee eht • vahs thrihn • khun geh • huhn
Would you like to go out for dinner?	**Möchten Sie mit mir etwas essen gehen?**
	merkht • uhn zee eht • vahs ehs • suhn geh • huhn
What are your plans for... ?	**Was haben Sie ... vor?**
	vahs <u>hah</u> • buhn zee ... fohr
today	**heute**
	<u>hoy</u> • tuh
tonight	**heute Abend**
	<u>hoy</u> • tuh <u>ah</u> • buhnt
tomorrow	**morgen**
	<u>mohr</u> • guhn
this weekend	**dieses Wochenende**
	<u>dee</u> • zuhs voh • <u>khuhn</u> • ehn • duh
Where would you like to go?	**Wohin möchten Sie gern gehen?**
	<u>voh</u> • hihn merkh • tuhn zee gehrn <u>geh</u> • uhn
I'd like to go...	**Ich möchte gern ... gehen.**
	eekh <u>merkh</u> • tuh gehrn ... <u>geh</u> • uhn
Do you like...?	**Mögen Sie ...?**
	<u>mer</u> • guhn zee ...
Can I have your number/e-mail?	**Kann ich Ihre Telefonnummer/E-Mail haben?**
	kahn eekh <u>ee</u> • ruh teh • leh • <u>fohn</u> • noo • mehr/<u>ee</u> • mehl <u>hah</u> • buhn
Are you on Facebook/Twitter?	**Sind Sie bei Facebook/Twitter?**
	(polite form)
	zihnt zee by face • book/twit • ter
Can I join you?	**Kann ich mitkommen?**
	kahn eekh <u>miht</u> • koh • muhn

You're very attractive.	**Sie sind sehr attraktiv.**
	zee zihnt zehr aht • rahk • teef
Let's go somewhere quieter.	**Lassen Sie uns an einen ruhigeren Ort gehen.**
	lah • suhn zee oons ahn ien • uhn
	roo • ee • geh • ruhn ohrt geh • uhn

For Communications, see page 86.

ACCEPTING & REJECTING

I'd love to.	**Gerne.**
	gehr • nuh
Where should we meet?	**Wo wollen wir uns treffen?**
	voh voh • luhn veer oons treh • fuhn
I'll meet you at the bar/your hotel.	**Ich treffe Sie an der Bar/Ihrem Hotel.**
	eekh treh • fuh zee ahn dehr bahr/
	ee • ruhm hoh • tehl
I'll come by at…	**Ich komme um … vorbei.**
	eekh koh • muh oom … fohr • bie
What is your address?	**Wie ist Ihre Adresse?**
	vee ihst ee • ruh ah • drehs • uh
I'm busy.	**Ich bin beschäftigt.**
	eekh been beh • shehf • teekt
I'm not interested.	**Ich habe kein Interesse.**
	eekh hah • buh kien ihn • teh • reh • suh
Leave me alone.	**Lassen Sie mich in Ruhe.**
	lah • sehn zee meekh ihn roo • uh
Stop bothering me!	**Hören Sie auf, mich zu belästigen!**
	her • ruhn zee owf meekh tsoo
	buh • lay • steeg • uhn

For Time, see page 25.

GETTING INTIMATE

Can I hug/kiss you?	**Kann ich dich umarmen/küssen?**
	kahn eekh deekh <u>oom</u> • ahr • muhn/<u>kew</u> • zuhn
Yes.	**Ja.**
	yah
No.	**Nein.**
	nien
Stop!	**Stopp!**
	shtohp
I like/love you.	**Ich mag/liebe dich.**
	eekh mahk/<u>lee</u> • buh deekh

SEXUAL PREFERENCES

Are you gay?	**Bist du schwul?**
	beesht doo shvool
I'm...	**Ich bin ...**
	eekh been ...
heterosexual	**heterosexuell**
	heh • tuh • roh • <u>schks</u> • oo • ehl
homosexual	**homosexuell**
	hoh • moh • <u>sehks</u> • oo • ehl
bisexual	**bisexuell**
	bee • <u>sehks</u> • oo • ehl
Do you like men/ women?	**Magst du Männer/Frauen?**
	mahgst doo <u>meh</u> • nehr/<u>frow</u> • uhn

DICTIONARY

ENGLISH–GERMAN

A

accept v akzeptieren
access n der Zutritt
accident der Unfall
accommodation die Unterkunft
account n (bank) das Konto
acupuncture die Akupunktur
adapter der Adapter
address n die Adresse
admission (price) der Eintritt
after nach; ~**noon** der Nachmittag; ~**shave** das Aftershave
age n das Alter
agency die Agentur
AIDS AIDS
air n die Luft; ~ **conditioning** die Klimaanlage; ~**-dry** lufttrocknen; ~ **pump** die Luftpumpe; ~**line** die Fluggesellschaft; ~**mail** die Luftpost; ~**plane** das Flugzeug; ~**port** der Flughafen
aisle der Gang; ~ **seat** der Platz am Gang

allergic allergisch; ~ **reaction** die allergische Reaktion
allow erlauben
alone allein
alter v umändern
alternate route die Alternativroute
aluminum foil die Aluminiumfolie
amazing erstaunlich
ambulance der Krankenwagen
American adj amerikanisch
amusement park der Vergnügungspark
anemic anämisch
anesthesia die Anästhesie
animal das Tier
ankle das Fußgelenk
antibiotic n das Antibiotikum
antiques store das Antiquitätengeschäft
antiseptic cream die antiseptische Creme
apartment das Apartment
appendix (body part) der Blinddarm

---

adj adjective	**BE** British English	**prep** prepostion
adv adverb	**n** noun	**v** verb

appetizer die Vorspeise
appointment der Termin
arcade die Spielhalle
area code die Ortsvorwahl
arm n (body part) der Arm
aromatherapy die Aromatherapie
around (the corner) um; ~ (price) ungefähr
arrival Ankunft
arrive ankommen
artery die Arterie
arthritis die Arthritis
art die Kunst
Asian adj asiatisch
aspirin das Aspirin
asthmatic asthmatisch
ATM der Bankautomat; ~ card die Bankkarte
attack v angreifen
attraction (place) die Sehenswürdigkeit
attractive attraktiv
Australia das Australien
Australian adj australisch
automatic automatisch; ~ car das Auto mit Automatikschaltung
available verfügbar

B

baby das Baby; ~ bottle die Babyflasche; ~ wipe das Baby-Pflegetuch; ~sitter der Babysitter

back (body part) der Rücken; ~ache die Rückenschmerzen; ~pack der Rucksack
bag die Tasche
baggage [BE] das Gepäck; ~ claim die Gepäckausgabe; ~ ticket der Gepäckschein
bake v backen
bakery die Bäckerei
ballet das Ballett
bandage das Pflaster
bank n die Bank
bar (place) die Bar
barbecue (device) n der Grill
barber der Herrenfriseur
baseball der Baseball
basket (grocery store) der Einkaufskorb
basketball der Basketball
bathroom das Bad
battery die Batterie
battleground das Schlachtfeld
be v sein
beach der Strand
beautiful wunderschön; ~ schön
bed n das Bett; ~ and breakfast die Pension
before vor
begin beginnen
beginner der Anfänger
behind (direction) hinter

beige *adj* beige

belt der Gürtel

best *adj* beste; **~ before** mindestens haltbar bis

better besser

bicycle das Fahrrad

big groß; **~ger** größerger

bike route die Radroute

bikini der Bikini

bill *n* **(money)** der Geldschein; **~** *n* **(of sale)** die Rechnung

bird der Vogel

birthday der Geburtstag

black *adj* schwarz

bladder die Blase

bland fad

blanket die Decke

bleed bluten

blender der Mixer

blood das Blut; **~ pressure** der Blutdruck

blouse die Bluse

blue *adj* blau

board *v* einsteigen; **~ing pass** die Bordkarte

boat *n* das Boot

boil *v* kochen

bone *n* der Knochen

book *n* das Buch; **~store** der Buchladen

boot *n* der Stiefel

boring langweilig

botanical garden der botanische Garten

bother *v* belästigen

bottle *n* die Flasche; **~ opener** der Flaschenöffner

bowl *n* die Schüssel

boxing match der Boxkampf

boy der Junge; **~friend** der Freund

bra der BH

bracelet das Armband

brake (car) die Bremse

breaded paniert

break *v* **(bone)** brechen

breakdown (car) die Panne

breakfast *n* das Frühstück

break-in (burglary) *n* der Einbruch

breast die Brust; **~feed** *v* stillen

breathe atmen

bridge die Brücke

briefs (clothing) der Schlüpfer

bring bringen

British *adj* britisch

broken kaputt; **~ (bone)** gebrochen

brooch die Brosche

broom der Besen

brother der Bruder

brown *adj* braun

bug (insect) *n* das Insekt

building das Gebäude

burn *v* brennen

bus *n* der Bus; **~ station** der Busbahnhof; **~ stop** die Bushaltestelle;

~ **ticket** die Busfahrkarte;
~ **tour** die Busreise
business *adj* Geschäfts-;
~ **card** die Visitenkarte;
~ **center** das
Geschäftszentrum;
~ **class** die Business-Class;
~ **hours** die Öffnungszeiten
butcher *n* der Fleischer
buttocks der Po
buy *v* kaufen
bye auf Wiedersehen

C

cabaret das Kabarett
cable car die Seilbahn
cafe (place) das Café
call *v* **(phone)** anrufen;
~ *n* der Anruf ~ **collect** ein
R-Gespräch führen
calorie die Kalorie
camera die Kamera;
~ **case** die Kameratasche;
digital ~ die Digitalkamera
camp *v* campen; ~**ing stove**
der Campingkocher;
~**site** der Campingplatz
can opener der Dosenöffner
Canada das Kanada
Canadian *adj* kanadisch
cancel stornieren
candy die Süßigkeit
canned good die Konserve
canyon der Canyon
car das Auto;

~ **hire [BE]** die
Autovermietung; ~ **park [BE]**
der Parkplatz;
~ **rental** die Autovermietung;
~ **seat** der Autositz
carafe die Karaffe
card *n* die Karte;
ATM ~ die Bankkarte;
credit ~ die Kreditkarte;
debit ~ dle EC-Karte;
phone ~ die Telefonkarte
carry-on *n* **(piece of hand
luggage)** das
Handgepäckstück
cart (grocery store) der
Einkaufswagen; ~ **(luggage)**
der Gepäckwagen
carton (of cigarettes) die
Stange (Zigaretten);
~ **(of groceries)** die Packung
cash *n* das Bargeld;
~ *v* einlösen
cashier der Kassierer
casino das Casino
castle das Schloss
cathedral die Kathedrale
cave *n* die Höhle
CD die CD
cell phone das Handy
Celsius Celsius
centimeter der Zentimeter
certificate das Zertifikat
chair *n* der Stuhl;
~ **lift** der Sessellift
change *v* **(baby)** wickeln;

~ **(buses)** umsteigen;
~ **(money)** wechseln;
~ *n* **(money)** das
Wechselgeld
charge *v* **(credit card)**
belasten; ~ **(cost)** verlangen
cheap billig; ~**er** billiger
check *v* **(luggage)**
aufgeben; ~ **(on something)**
prüfen; *n* **(payment)** der
Scheck; ~~**in** das Check-in;
~**ing account** das Girokonto;
~~**out** das Check-out
Cheers! Prost!
chemical toilet die
Campingtoilette
chemist [BE] die Apotheke
chest (body part) die Brust;
~ **pain** die Brustschmerzen
chewing gum der Kaugummi
child das Kind;
~**'s seat** der Kinderstuhl
children's menu das
Kindermenü
children's portion die
Kinderportion
Chinese *adj* chinesisch
chopsticks die Stäbchen
church die Kirche
cigar die Zigarre
cigarette die Zigarette
class *n* die Klasse;
business ~ die Business-
Class; **economy** ~ die
Economy-Class; **first** ~ die

erste Klasse
classical music die
klassische Musik
clean *v* reinigen; ~ *adj*
(clothes) sauber;
~**ing product** das
Reinigungsmittel
clear *v* **(on an ATM)** löschen
cliff die Klippe
cling film [BE] die
Klarsichtfolie
close *v* **(a shop)** schließen
closed geschlossen
clothing die Bekleidung;
~ **store** das
Bekleidungsgeschäft
club *n* der Club
coat der Mantel
coin die Münze
colander das Sieb
cold *n* **(sickness)** die
Erkältung; ~ *adj*
(temperature) kalt
colleague der Kollege
cologne das Kölnischwasser
color *n* die Farbe
comb *n* der Kamm
come *v* kommen
complaint die Beschwerde
computer der Computer
concert das Konzert;
~ **hall** die Konzerthalle
condition (medical) die
Beschwerden
conditioner (hair) die

Spülung
condom das Kondom
conference die Konferenz
confirm bestätigen
congestion (medical) der Blutstau
connect (internet) verbinden
connection (travel/internet) die Verbindung; **~ flight** der Anschlussflug
constipated verstopft
consulate das Konsulat
consultant der Berater
contact v kontaktieren
contact lens die Kontaktlinse; **~ solution** Kontaktlinsenlösung
contagious ansteckend
convention hall der Kongresssaal
conveyor belt das Förderband
cook v kochen
cool adj **(temperature)** kalt
copper n das Kupfer
corkscrew n der Korkenzieher
cost v kosten
cotton die Baumwolle
cough v husten; **~ n** der Husten
country code die Landesvorwahl
cover charge der Preis pro Gedeck

cream (ointment) die Creme
credit card die Kreditkarte
crew neck der runde Halsausschnitt
crib das Kinderbett
crystal n **(glass)** das Kristall
cup n die Tasse
currency die Währung; **~ exchange** der Währungsumtausch; **~ exchange office** die Wechselstube
current account [BE] das Girokonto
customs der Zoll
cut v schneiden; **~ n (injury)** der Schnitt
cute süß
cycling das Radfahren

D

damage v beschädigen
dance v tanzen; **~ club** der Tanzclub; **~ing** das Tanzen
dangerous gefährlich
dark adj dunkel
date n **(calendar)** das Datum
day der Tag
deaf adj taub
debit card die EC-Karte
deck chair der Liegestuhl
declare v **(customs)** deklarieren
decline v **(credit card)** ablehnen

deep *adj* tief
degree (temperature) das
Grad
delay *v* verzögern
delete *v* **(computer)** löschen
delicatessen das
Feinkostgeschäft
delicious lecker
denim das Denim
dentist der Zahnarzt
denture die Zahnprothese
deodorant das Deodorant
department store das
Kaufhaus
departure (plane) der Abflug
deposit *v* **(money)** einzahlen;
~ *n* **(bank)** die Einzahlung
desert *n* die Wüste
detergent das Waschmittel
develop *v* **(film)** entwickeln
diabetic *adj* diabetisch; *n* der
Diabetiker
dial *v* wählen
diamond der Diamant
diaper die Windel
diarrhea der Durchfall
diesel der Diesel
difficult schwierig
digital digital; ~ **camera**
die Digitalkamera;
~ **photo** das Digitalfoto;
~ **print** der digitale Ausdruck
dining room das Esszimmer
dinner das Abendessen
direction die Richtung

dirty schmutzig
disabled *adj* **(person)**
behindert; ~ **accessible [BE]**
behindertengerecht
disconnect
(computer) trennen
discount *n* der Rabatt; die
Ermäßigung
dishes (kitchen) das Geschirr
dishwasher der
Geschirrspüler
dishwashing liquid
das Geschirrspülmittel
display *n* **(device)** das
Display; ~ **case** die Vitrine
disposable *n* der
Einwegartikel; ~ **razor** der
Einweg-Rasierer
dive *v* tauchen
diving equipment
die Tauchausrüstung
divorce *v* sich scheiden
lassen
dizzy *adj* schwindelig
doctor *n* der Arzt
doll *n* die Puppe
dollar (U.S.) der Dollar
domestic inländisch;
~ **flight** der Inlandsflug
door die Tür
dormitory der Schlafsaal
double bed das Doppelbett
downtown *n* das
Stadtzentrum
dozen das Dutzend

drag lift der Schlepplift
dress (clothing) das Kleid;
~ **code** die Kleiderordnung
drink v trinken; ~ n das
Getränk; ~ **menu** die
Getränkekarte; **~ing water**
das Trinkwasser
drive v fahren
driver's license number die
Führerscheinnummer
drop n **(medicine)** der Tropfen
drowsiness die Schläfrigkeit
dry clean chemisch reinigen;
~er's die chemische
Reinigung
dubbed synchronisiert
during während
duty (tax) der Zoll; **~-free**
zollfrei
DVD die DVD

E

ear das Ohr; **~ache** die
Ohrenschmerzen
earlier früher
early früh
earring der Ohrring
east n der Osten
easy leicht
eat v essen
economy class die Economy-
Class
elbow n der Ellenbogen
electric outlet die Steckdose
elevator der Fahrstuhl

e-mail v eine E-Mail senden;
~ n die E-Mail; ~ **address** die
E-Mail-Adresse
emergency der Notfall;
~ **exit** der Notausgang
empty v entleeren
end v beenden; ~ n das Ende
engaged (person) verlobt
English adj englisch; ~ n
(language) das Englisch
engrave eingravieren
enjoy genießen
enter v **(place)** eintreten
entertainment die
Unterhaltung
entrance der Eingang
envelope der Umschlag
epileptic adj epileptisch;
~ n der Epileptiker
equipment die Ausrüstung
escalator die Rolltreppe
e-ticket das E-Ticket
EU resident der EU-Bürger
euro der Euro
evening n der Abend
excess baggage das
Übergepäck
exchange v umtauschen;
~ n **(place)** die
Wechselstube; ~ **rate** der
Wechselkurs
excursion der Ausflug
excuse v entschuldigen
exhausted erschöpft
exit v verlassen; ~ n der

Ausgang

expensive teuer

experienced erfahren

expert der Experte

exposure (film) die Belichtung

express *adj* Express-; **~ bus** der Expressbus; **~ train** der Expresszug

extension (phone) die Durchwahl

extra *adj* zusätzlich; **~ large** extragroß

extract *v* **(tooth)** ziehen

eye das Auge

eyebrow wax die Augenbrauenkorrektur

F

face *n* das Gesicht

facial *n* die kosmetische Gesichtsbehandlung

family *n* die Familie

fan *n* **(appliance)** der Ventilator

far (distance) weit

farm der Bauernhof

far-sighted weitsichtig

fast *adj* schnell

fat free fettfrei

father der Vater

fax *v* faxen; **~** *n* das Fax; **~ number** die Faxnummer

fee *n* die Gebühr

feed *v* füttern

ferry *n* die Fähre

fever *n* das Fieber

field (sports) der Platz

fill *v* **(car)** tanken

fill out *v* **(form)** ausfüllen

filling *n* **(tooth)** die Füllung

film *n* **(camera)** der Film

fine *n* **(fee for breaking law)** die Strafe

finger *n* der Finger; **~nail** der Fingernagel

fire *n* das Feuer; **~ department** die Feuerwehr; **~ door** die Feuertür

first *adj* erste; **~ class** erste Klasse

fit *n* **(clothing)** die Passform

fitting room die Umkleidekabine

fix *v* **(repair)** reparieren

fixed-price menu das Festpreismenü

flash photography das Fotografieren mit Blitzlicht

flashlight das Blitzlicht

flight *n* der Flug

flip-flops die Badelatschen

floor *n* **(level)** die Etage

florist der Florist

flower *n* die Blume

folk music die Volksmusik

food das Essen; **~ processor** die Küchenmaschine

foot *n* der Fuß

football game [BE]
das Fußballspiel
for für
forecast *n* die Vorhersage
forest *n* der Wald
fork *n* die Gabel
form *n* **(document)** das
Formular
formula (baby) die
Babynahrung
fort die Festung
fountain *n* der Springbrunnen
free *adj* frei
freelance work die
freiberufliche Arbeit
freezer der Gefrierschrank
fresh frisch
friend der Freund
frozen food die Tiefkühlkost
frying pan die Bratpfanne
full-time *adj* Vollzeit-

G

game *n* das Spiel
garage *n* **(parking)** die
Garage; ~ *n* **(for repairs)** die
Autowerkstatt
garbage bag der Abfallbeutel
gas (car) das Benzin;
~ **station** die Tankstelle
gate (airport) das Gate
gay *adj* **(homosexual)** schwul;
~ **bar** die Schwulenbar;
~ **club** der Schwulenclub
gel *n* **(hair)** das Gel

generic drug das Generikum
German *adj* deutsch; ~ *n*
(language) das Deutsch
Germany Deutschland
get off (a train/bus/
subway) aussteigen
gift *n* das Geschenk; ~ **shop**
der Geschenkwarenladen
girl das Mädchen; ~**friend**
die Freundin
give *v* geben
glass (drinking) das Glas;
~ **(material)** das Glas
glasses die Brille
go *v* **(somewhere)** gehen
gold *n* das Gold
golf *n* das Golf; ~ **course**
der Golfplatz; ~ **tournament**
das Golfturnier
good *adj* gut; ~ *n* die Ware;
~ **afternoon** guten Tag
~ **day** guten Tag; ~ **evening**
guten Abend; ~ **morning**
guten Morgen; ~**bye** auf
Wiedersehen
gram das Gramm
grandchild das Enkelkind
grandparents die Großeltern
gray *adj* grau
green *adj* grün
grocery store das
Lebensmittelgeschäft
ground floor das Erdgeschoss
groundcloth die
Unterlegplane

group n die Gruppe
guide n (book) der Reiseführer; ~ n (person) der Fremdenführer ~ dog der Blindenhund
gym n (place) der Fitnessraum
gynecologist der Gynäkologe

H

hair das Haar; ~brush die Haarbürste; ~cut der Haarschnitt; ~ dryer der Fön; ~ salon der Friseursalon; ~spray das Haarspray; ~style die Frisur; ~ stylist der Friseur
halal halal
half adj halb; ~ n die Hälfte; ~ hour die halbe Stunde; ~-kilo das halbe Kilo
hammer n der Hammer
hand n die Hand; ~ luggage das Handgepäck; ~ wash die Handwäsche; ~bag [BE] die Handtasche
handicapped behindert; ~-accessible behindertengerecht
hangover der Kater
happy glücklich
hat der Hut
have v haben; ~ sex Sex haben

hay fever der Heuschnupfen
head (body part) n der Kopf; ~ache die Kopfschmerzen; ~phones die Kopfhörer
health die Gesundheit; ~ food store das Reformhaus
hearing impaired hörgeschädigt
heart das Herz; ~ condition die Herzkrankheit
heat v heizen; ~er das Heizgerät; ~ing [BE] die Heizung
hectare der Hektar
hello Hallo
helmet der Helm
help v helfen; ~ n die Hilfe
here hier
hi Hallo
high hoch; ~chair der Kindersitz; ~lights (hair) die Strähnchen; ~way die Autobahn
hiking boots die Wanderschuhe
hill n der Berg
hire v [BE] (a car) mieten; ~ car [BE] das Mietauto
hockey das Hockey
holiday [BE] der Urlaub
horsetrack die Pferderennbahn
hospital das Krankenhaus
hostel die Jugendherberge
hot (spicy) scharf;

~ (temperature) heiß;
~ spring heiße Quelle;
~ water heißes Wasser
hotel das Hotel
hour die Stunde
house n das Haus; ~hold
goods die Haushaltswaren;
~keeping services der
Hotelservice
how wie; ~ much wie viel
hug v umarmen
hungry hungrig
hurt v wehtun
husband der Ehemann

I

ibuprofen das Ibuprofen
ice n das Eis; ~ hockey das
Eishockey
icy eisig
identification die
Identifikation
ill krank
in in
include v beinhalten
indoor pool (public) das
Hallenbad
inexpensive preisgünstig
infected infiziert
information (phone) die
Auskunft; ~ desk die
Information
insect das Insekt: ~ bite der
Insektenstich; ~ repellent
der Insektenschutz

insert v (card) einführen
insomnia die Schlaflosigkeit
instant message die instant
Message
insulin das Insulin
insurance die Versicherung;
~ card die
Versicherungskarte;
~ company die
Versicherungsgesellschaft
interesting interessant
intermediate fortgeschritten
international international;
~ flight der internationale
Flug; ~ student card
der internationale
Studentenausweis
internet das Internet;
~ cafe das Internetcafé;
~ service der Internetservice
interpreter der Dolmetscher
intersection die Kreuzung
intestine der Darm
introduce v
(person) vorstellen
invoice n [BE] die Rechnung
Ireland das Irland
Irish adj irisch
iron v bügeln; ~ n
(clothes) das Bügeleisen
Italian adj italienisch

J

jacket n die Jacke
Japanese adj japanisch

jar n **(for jam etc.)** das Glas
jaw n der Kiefer
jazz n der Jazz; ~ **club** der Jazzclub
jeans die Jeans
jet ski n die Jet-Ski
jeweler der Juwelier
jewelry der Schmuck
join v **(go with somebody)** mitkommen
joint n **(body part)** das Gelenk

K

key n der Schlüssel; ~ **card** die Schlüsselkarte; ~**ring** der Schlüsselring
kiddie pool das Kinderbecken
kidney (body part) die Niere
kilo das Kilo; ~**gram** das Kilogramm; ~**meter** der Kilometer
kiss v küssen
kitchen die Küche; ~ **foil [BE]** die Aluminiumfolie
knee n das Knie
knife das Messer
kosher adj koscher

L

lace n **(fabric)** die Spitze
lactose intolerant laktoseintolerant
lake der See
large groß

last adj letzte
late (time) spät
launderette [BE] der Waschsalon
laundromat der Waschsalon
laundry (place) die Wäscherei ~ **service** der Wäscheservice
lawyer n der Anwalt
leather n das Leder
leave v **(hotel)** abreisen; ~ **(plane)** abfliegen
left adj, adv **(direction)** links
leg n das Bein
lens die Linse
less weniger
lesson n die Lektion; **take ~s** Unterricht nehmen
letter n der Brief
library die Bücherei
life jacket die Schwimmweste
lifeguard der Rettungsschwimmer
lift n **[BE]** der Fahrstuhl; ~ n **(ride)** die Mitfahrgelegenheit; ~ **pass** der Liftpass
light n **(cigarette)** das Feuer; ~ n **(overhead)** die Lampe; ~**bulb** die Glühbirne
lighter n das Feuerzeug
like v mögen
line n **(train/bus)** die Linie
linen das Leinen
lip n die Lippe

liquor store das Spirituosengeschäft
liter der Liter
little wenig
live v leben; ~ **music** Livemusik
liver (body part) die Leber
loafers die Halbschuhe
local n **(person)** der Einheimische
lock v abschließen; ~ n das Schloss
locker das Schließfach
log off v **(computer)** abmelden
log on v **(computer)** anmelden
long adj lang; ~-**sighted** [BE] weitsichtig; ~-**sleeved** langärmlig
look v schauen; ~ **for something** etwas suchen
loose (fit) locker
lose v **(something)** verlieren
lost verloren; ~-**and-found** das Fundbüro
lotion die Lotion
louder lauter
love v **(someone)** lieben; ~ n die Liebe
low adj niedrig
luggage das Gepäck; ~ **cart** der Gepäckwagen; ~ **locker** das Gepäckschließfach; ~ **ticket** der Gepäckschein

lunch n das Mittagessen
lung die Lunge
luxury car das Luxusauto

M

machine washable maschinenwaschbar
magazine das Magazin
magnificent großartig
mail v mit der Post schicken; ~ n die Post; ~**box** der Briefkasten
main attraction die Hauptattraktion
main course das Hauptgericht
mall das Einkaufszentrum
man (adult male) der Mann
manager der Manager
manicure n die Maniküre
manual car das Auto mit Gangschaltung
map n die Karte; ~ n **(town)** der Stadtplan
market n der Markt
married verheiratet
marry heiraten
mass n **(church service)** die Messe
massage n die Massage
match n das Spiel
meal die Mahlzeit
measure v **(someone)** Maß nehmen
measuring cup der

Messbecher

measuring spoon der Messlöffel

mechanic n der Mechaniker

medication (drugs) die Medikamente

medicine das Medikament

medium (steak) medium

meet v treffen

meeting n **(business)** das Meeting; ~ **room** das Konferenzzimmer

membership card der Mitgliedsausweis

memorial (place) das Denkmal

memory card die Speicherkarte

mend v **(clothes)** ausbessern

menstrual cramps die Menstruationskrämpfe

menu (restaurant) die Speisekarte

message die Nachricht

meter n **(parking)** die Parkuhr; ~ n **(measure)** der Meter

microwave n die Mikrowelle

midday [BE] der Mittag

midnight die Mitternacht

mileage die Meilenzahl

mini-bar die Mini-Bar

minute die Minute

missing (not there) weg

mistake n der Fehler

mobile home der Wohnwagen

mobile phone [BE] das Handy

mobility die Mobilität

monastery das Kloster

money das Geld

month der Monat

mop n der Wischmopp

moped das Moped

more mehr

morning n der Morgen

mosque die Moschee

mother n die Mutter

motion sickness die Reisekrankheit

motor n der Motor; ~ **boat** das Motorboot; ~**cycle** das Motorrad; ~**way [BE]** die Autobahn

mountain der Berg; ~ **bike** das Mountainbike

mousse (hair) der Schaumfestiger

mouth n der Mund

movie der Film; ~ **theater** das Kino

mug v überfallen

multiple-trip ticket der Mehrfachfahrschein

muscle n der Muskel

museum das Museum

music die Musik; ~ **store** das Musikgeschäft

N

nail file die Nagelfeile
nail salon das Nagelstudio
name n der Name
napkin die Serviette
nappy [BE] die Windel
nationality die Nationalität
nature preserve das Naturreservat
nausea die Übelkeit
nauseous übel
near nahe; **~-sighted** kurzsichtig
nearby in der Nähe von
neck n der Nacken
necklace die Kette
need v brauchen
newspaper die Zeitung
newsstand der Zeitungskiosk
next adj nächste
nice schön
night die Nacht; **~club** der Nachtclub
no nein; **~ (not any)** kein
non-alcoholic nichtalkoholisch
non-smoking adj Nichtraucher
noon n der Mittag
north n der Norden
nose die Nase
note n [BE] (money) der Geldschein
nothing nichts
notify v benachrichtigen
novice der Anfänger
now jetzt
number n die Nummer
nurse n die Krankenschwester

O

office das Büro; **~ hours** die Bürozeiten
off-licence [BE] das Spirituosengeschäft
oil n das Öl
OK okay
old adj alt
on the corner an der Ecke
once (one time) einmal
one ein; **(counting)** eins; **~-day (ticket)** Tages-; **~-way ticket (airline)** das einfache Ticket, **(bus/train/subway)** die Einzelfahrkarte; **~-way street** die Einbahnstraße
only nur
open v öffnen; **~** adj offen
opera die Oper; **~ house** das Opernhaus
opposite n das Gegenteil
optician der Optiker
orange adj (color) orange
orchestra das Orchester
order v (restaurant) bestellen
outdoor pool das Freibad
outside prep draußen

over *prep* (direction) über;
  ~done (meat) zu lang
  gebraten; **~heat** *v* (car)
  überhitzen; **~look** *n*
  (scenic place) der
  Aussichtsplatz; **~night**
  über Nacht; **~-the-counter**
  (medication) rezeptfrei
oxygen treatment
  die Sauerstoffbehandlung

P

p.m. nachmittags
pacifier der Schnuller
pack *v* packen
package *n* das Paket
pad *n* [BE] die Monatsbinde
paddling pool [BE]
  das Kinderbecken
pain der Schmerz
pajamas der Pyjama
palace der Palast
pants die Hose
pantyhose die Strumpfhose
paper *n* (material) das
  Papier; **~ towel** das
  Papierhandtuch
paracetamol [BE] das
  Paracetamol
park *v* parken; **~** *n* der Park;
  ~ing garage das Parkhaus;
  ~ing lot der Parkplatz;
  ~ing meter die Parkuhr
parliament building
  das Parlamentsgebäude

part (for car) das Teil;
  ~-time *adj* Teilzeit-
pass through *v* (travel)
  durchreisen
passenger der Passagier
passport der Reisepass;
  ~ control die Passkontrolle
password das Passwort
pastry shop die Konditorei
patch *v* (clothing) ausbessern
path der Pfad
pay *v* bezahlen; **~phone**
  das öffentliche Telefon
peak *n* der Gipfel
pearl *n* die Perle
pedestrian *n* der Fußgänger
pediatrician der Kinderarzt
pedicure *n* die Pediküre
pen *n* der Stift
penicillin das Penicillin
penis der Penis
per pro; **~ day** pro Tag;
  ~ hour pro Stunde;
  ~ night pro Nacht;
  ~ week pro Woche
perfume *n* das Parfüm
period (menstrual) die
  Periode; **~ (of time)** der
  Zeitraum
permit *v* erlauben
petrol [BE] das Benzin;
  ~ station [BE] die Tankstelle
pewter das Zinn
pharmacy die Apotheke
phone *v* anrufen; **~** *n* das

Telefon; **~ call** das Telefonat;
~ card die Telefonkarte;
~ number die
Telefonnummer
photo das Foto; **~copy** die
Fotokopie;
~graphy die Fotografie
pick up *v* **(person)** abholen
picnic area der Rastplatz
piece *n* das Stück
Pill (birth control) die Pille
pillow *n* das Kissen
pink *adj* rosa
piste [BE] die Piste; **~ map**
[BE] der Pistenplan
pizzeria die Pizzeria
place *v* **(a bet)** abgeben
plane *n* das Flugzeug
plastic wrap die Klarsichtfolie
plate *n* der Teller
platform [BE] (train) der
Bahnsteig
platinum *n* das Platin
play *v* spielen; **~** *n* **(theatre)**
das Stück; **~ground** der
Spielplatz; **~pen** der
Laufstall
please *adv* bitte
pleasure *n* die Freude
plunger die Saugglocke
plus size die Übergröße
pocket *n* die Tasche
poison *n* das Gift
poles (skiing) die Stöcke
police die Polizei;

~ report der Polizeibericht;
~ station das Polizeirevier
pond *n* der Teich
pool *n* der Pool
pop music die Popmusik
portion *n* die Portion
post *n* **[BE]** die Post;
~ office die Post;
~box [BE] der Briefkasten;
~card [BE] die Postkarte
pot *n* der Topf
pottery die Töpferwaren
pound *n* **(weight)** das Pfund;
~ (British sterling) das
Pfund
pregnant schwanger
prescribe (medication)
verschreiben
prescription das Rezept
press *v* **(clothing)** bügeln
price *n* der Preis
print *v* drucken; **~** *n* der
Ausdruck
problem das Problem
produce *n* das Erzeugnis;
~ store das
Lebensmittelgeschäft
prohibit verbieten
pronounce aussprechen
Protestant der Protestant
public *adj* öffentlich
pull *v* ziehen
purple *adj* violett
purse *n* die Handtasche
push *v* drücken; **~chair [BE]**

der Kinderwagen

Q

quality *n* die Qualität
question *n* die Frage
quiet *adj* leise

R

racetrack die Rennbahn
racket *n* (**sports**) der
   Schläger
railway station [BE] der
   Bahnhof
rain *n* der Regen; ~**coat** die
   Regenjacke; ~**forest** der
   Regenwald; ~**y** regnerisch
rap *n* (**music**) der Rap
rape *v* vergewaltigen;
   ~ *n* die Vergewaltigung
rare selten
rash *n* der Ausschlag
ravine die Schlucht
razor blade die Rasierklinge
reach *v* erreichen
ready bereit
real *adj* echt
receipt *n* die Quittung
receive *v* erhalten
reception (**hotel**) die
   Rezeption
recharge *v* aufladen
recommend empfehlen
recommendation die
   Empfehlung
recycling das Recycling

red *adj* rot
refrigerator der Kühlschrank
region die Region
registered mail das
   Einschreiben
regular *n* (**fuel**) das
   Normalbenzin
relationship die Beziehung
rent *v* mieten; ~ *n* die Miete
rental car das Mietauto
repair *v* reparieren
repeat *v* wiederholen
reservation die Reservierung;
   ~ **desk** der
   Reservierungsschalter
reserve *v* (**hotel**) reservieren
restaurant das Restaurant
restroom die Toilette
retired *adj* (**from work**) in
   Rente
return *v* (**something**)
   zurückgeben; ~ *n* [BE] (**trip**)
   die Hin- und Rückfahrt
reverse *v* (**the charges**) [BE]
   ein R-Gespräch führen
rib *n* (**body part**) die Rippe
right *adj*, *adv*
   (**direction**) rechts; ~ **of**
   way die Vorfahrt
ring *n* der Ring
river der Fluss
road map die Straßenkarte
rob *v* berauben
robbed beraubt
romantic *adj* romantisch

room n das Zimmer; **~ key** der Zimmerschlüssel; **~ service** der Zimmerservice
round trip die Hin- und Rückfahrt
route n die Route
rowboat das Ruderboot
rubbing alcohol der Franzbranntwein
rubbish n [BE] der Abfall; **~ bag** [BE] der Abfallbeutel
rugby das Rugby
ruin n die Ruine
rush n die Eile

S

sad traurig
safe adj (protected) sicher; **~** n (thing) der Safe
sales tax die Mehrwertsteuer
same adj gleiche
sandals die Sandalen
sanitary napkin die Monatsbinde
sauna die Sauna
sauté v sautieren
save v (computer) speichern
savings (account) das Sparkonto
scanner der Scanner
scarf der Schal
schedule v planen; **~** n der Plan
school n die Schule
science die Wissenschaft

scissors die Schere
sea das Meer
seat n der Sitzplatz
security die Sicherheit
see v sehen
self-service n die Selbstbedienung
sell v verkaufen
seminar das Seminar
send v senden
senior citizen der Rentner
separated (person) getrennt lebend
serious ernst
service (in a restaurant) die Bedienung
sexually transmitted disease (STD) die sexuell übertragbare Krankheit
shampoo n das Shampoo
sharp adj scharf
shaving cream die Rasiercreme
sheet n (bed) die Bettwäsche
ship v versenden
shirt das Hemd
shoe store das Schuhgeschäft
shoe der Schuh
shop v einkaufen; **~** n das Geschäft
shopping n das Einkaufen; **~ area** das Einkaufszentrum; **~ centre** [BE] das Einkaufszentrum;

~ mall das Einkaufszentrum
short kurz; **~-sleeved**
kurzärmelig
shorts die kurze Hose
short-sighted [BE] kurzsichtig
shoulder n die Schulter
show v zeigen
shower n **(bath)** die Dusche
shrine der Schrein
sick adj krank
side n die Seite; **~ dish**
die Beilage; **~ effect** die
Nebenwirkung; **~ order** die
Beilage
sightseeing das Besichtigen
von Sehenswürdigkeiten;
~ tour die Besichtigungstour
sign v
(document) unterschreiben
silk die Seide
silver n das Silber
single adj
(person) alleinstehend;
~ bed das Einzelbett;
~ print der Einzelabzug;
~ room das Einzelzimmer
sink n das Waschbecken
sister die Schwester
sit v sitzen
size n die Größe
ski v Ski fahren; **~** n der Ski;
~ lift der Skilift
skin n die Haut
skirt n der Rock
sleep v schlafen; **~er car**

der Schlafwagen; **~ing bag**
der Schlafsack; **~ing car [BE]**
der Schlafwagen
slice n die Scheibe
slippers die Pantoffeln
slower langsamer
slowly langsam
small klein
smoke v rauchen
smoking (area) Raucher-
snack bar der Imbiss
sneakers die Turnschuhe
snowboard n das Snowboard
snowshoe n der
Schneeschuh
snowy verschneit
soap n die Seife
soccer der Fußball
sock die Socke
some (with singular nouns)
etwas; **~ (with plural nouns)**
einige
soother [BE] der Schnuller
sore throat die
Halsschmerzen
south n der Süden
souvenir n das Souvenir;
~ store das Souvenirgeschäft
spa das Wellness-Center
spatula der Spatel
speak v sprechen
specialist (doctor) der
Spezialist
specimen die Probe
speeding die Geschwindig-

keitsüberschreitung
spell v buchstabieren
spicy scharf; ~ **(not bland)** würzig
spine (body part) die Wirbelsäule
spoon n der Löffel
sports der Sport; ~ **massage** die Sportmassage
sprain n die Verstauchung
stadium das Stadion
stairs die Treppe
stamp v **(ticket)** entwerten; ~ n **(postage)** die Briefmarke
start v beginnen
starter [BE] die Vorspeise
station n **(stop)** die Haltestelle; **bus ~** der Busbahnhof; **gas ~** die Tankstelle; **petrol ~** [BE] die Tankstelle; **subway ~** die U-Bahn-Haltestelle; **train ~** der Bahnhof
statue die Statue
steakhouse das Steakhouse
steal v stehlen
steep adj steil
sterling silver das Sterlingsilber
sting n der Stich
stolen gestohlen
stomach der Magen; ~**ache** die Bauchschmerzen

stool (bowel movement) der Stuhlgang
stop v **(bus)** anhalten; ~ n **(transportation)** die Haltestelle
store directory (mall) der Übersichtsplan
storey [BE] die Etage
stove n der Herd
straight adv **(direction)** geradeaus
strange seltsam
stream n der Strom
stroller (baby) der Kinderwagen
student (university) der Student; ~ **(school)** der Schüler
study v studieren; ~**ing** n das Studieren
stuffed gefüllt
stunning umwerfend
subtitle n der Untertitel
subway die U-Bahn; ~ **station** die U-Bahn Haltestelle
suit n der Anzug; ~**case** der Koffer
sun n die Sonne; ~**block** das Sonnenschutzmittel; ~**burn** der Sonnenbrand; ~**glasses** die Sonnenbrille; ~**ny** sonnig; ~**screen** die Sonnencreme; ~**stroke** der Sonnenstich
super n **(fuel)** das Superbenzin; ~**market** der

Supermarkt
surfboard das Surfboard
surgical spirit [BE] der Franzbranntwein
swallow v schlucken
sweater der Pullover
sweatshirt das Sweatshirt
sweet n **[BE]** die Süßigkeit; ~ adj **(taste)** süß
swelling die Schwellung
swim v schwimmen; ~**suit** der Badeanzug
symbol (keyboard) das Zeichen
synagogue die Synagoge

T

table n der Tisch
tablet (medicine) die Tablette
take v nehmen
tampon n der Tampon
taste v **(test)** kosten
taxi n das Taxi
team n das Team
teaspoon der Teelöffel
telephone n das Telefon
temple (religious) der Tempel
temporary vorübergehend
tennis das Tennis
tent n das Zelt; ~ **peg** der Zelthering; ~ **pole** die Zeltstange
terminal n **(airport)** der Terminal
terrible schrecklich

text v **(send a message)** eine SMS schicken; ~ n der Text
thank v danken; ~ **you** vielen Dank
the der?, das (neuter), die/
theater das Theater
theft der Diebstahl
there dort
thief der Dieb
thigh der Oberschenkel
thirsty durstig
this dieser?, dieses (neuter), diese/
throat der Hals
thunderstorm das Gewitter
ticket n die Fahrkarte; ~ **office** der Fahrkartenschalter
tie n **(clothing)** die Krawatte
tight (fit) eng
tights [BE] die Strumpfhose
time die Zeit; ~**table [BE] (transportation)** der Fahrplan
tire n der Reifen
tired müde
tissue das Gewebe
tobacconist der Tabakhändler
today adv heute
toe n der Zeh
toenail der Zehnagel
toilet [BE] die Toilette; ~ **paper** das Toilettenpapier

tomorrow adv morgen
tongue n die Zunge
tonight heute Abend
to (direction) zu
tooth der Zahn
toothpaste die Zahnpasta
total n (amount) der Gesamtbetrag
tough adj (food) zäh
tour n die Tour
tourist der Tourist; ~ **information office** das Touristeninformationsbüro
tow truck der Abschleppwagen
towel n das Handtuch
tower n der Turm
town die Stadt; ~ **hall** das Rathaus; ~ **map** der Stadtplan; ~ **square** der Rathausplatz
toy das Spielzeug; ~ **store** der Spielzeugladen
track n (train) der Bahnsteig
traditional traditionell
traffic light die Ampel
trail n (ski) die Piste; ~ **map** der Pistenplan
trailer (car) der Anhänger
train n der Zug; ~ **station** der Bahnhof
transfer v (change trains/ flights) umsteigen; ~ (money) überweisen
translate übersetzen

trash n der Abfall
travel n das Reisen; ~ **agency** das Reisebüro; ~ **sickness** die Reisekrankheit; ~**ers check** [**cheque** BE] der Reisescheck
tree der Baum
trim (hair) v nachschneiden
trip n die Reise
trolley [BE] (grocery store) der Einkaufswagen; ~ [BE] (luggage) der Gepäckwagen
trousers [BE] die Hose
T-shirt das T-Shirt
tumble dry maschinentrocknen
turn off v (device) ausschalten
turn on v (device) anschalten
TV der Fernseher
tyre [BE] der Reifen

U

ugly hässlich
umbrella der Regenschirm
unbranded medication [BE] das Generikum
unconscious (faint) bewusstlos
underdone halb gar
underground n [BE] die U-Bahn; ~ **station** [BE] die U-Bahn-Haltestelle
underpants [BE] der Slip

understand v verstehen
underwear die Unterwäsche
United Kingdom (U.K.)
das Großbritannien
United States (U.S.)
die Vereinigten Staaten
university die Universität
unleaded (gas) bleifrei
upset stomach
die Magenverstimmung
urgent dringend
urine der Urin
use v benutzen
username der Benutzername
utensil das Haushaltsgerät

V

vacancy (room) das freie
Zimmer
vacation der Urlaub
vaccination die Impfung
vacuum cleaner der
Staubsauger
vaginal infection die vaginale
Entzündung
valid gültig
valley das Tal
valuable adj wertvoll
value n der Wert
van der Kleintransporter
VAT [BE] die Mehrwertsteuer
vegan n der Veganer;
~ adj vegan
vegetarian n der Vegetarier;
~ adj vegetarisch

vehicle registration
die Fahrzeugregistrierung
viewpoint (scenic) [BE]
der Aussichtsplatz
village das Dorf
vineyard das Weingut
visa das Visum
visit v besuchen; **~ing hours**
die Besuchszeiten
visually
impaired sehbehindert
vitamin das Vitamin
V-neck der V-Ausschnitt
volleyball game das
Volleyballspiel
vomit v erbrechen;
~ing das Erbrechen

W

wait v warten;
~ n die Wartezeit
waiter der Kellner
waiting room der Warteraum
waitress die Kellnerin
wake v wecken;
~-up call der Weckruf
walk v spazieren gehen;
~ n der Spaziergang;
~ing route die Wanderroute
wallet die Geldbörse
war memorial
das Kriegsdenkmal
warm v
(something) erwärmen;
~ adj **(temperature)** warm

washing machine die Waschmaschine
watch v beobachten
waterfall der Wasserfall
wax v (hair) mit Wachs entfernen (Haare)
weather n das Wetter
week die Woche; **~end** das Wochenende
weekly wöchentlich
welcome adj willkommen; **you're ~** gern geschehen
west n der Westen
what was
wheelchair der Rollstuhl; **~ ramp** die Rollstuhlrampe
when adv (at what time) wann
where wo
white adj weiß; **~ gold** das Weißgold
who (question) wer
widowed verwitwet
wife die Ehefrau
window das Fenster; **~ case** das Schaufenster
wine list die Weinkarte

wireless wireless; **~ phone** das schnurlose Telefon
with mit
withdraw v (money) abheben; **~al** (bank) die Abhebung
without ohne
woman die Frau
wool die Wolle
work v arbeiten
wrap v einpacken
wrist das Handgelenk
write v schreiben

Y

year das Jahr
yellow adj gelb
yes ja
yesterday adv gestern
young adj jung
youth hostel die Jugendherberge

Z

zoo der Zoo

GERMAN–ENGLISH

A

der Abend evening
das Abendessen dinner
der Abfall n trash [rubbish BE]
der Abfallbeutel garbage [rubbish BE] bag
abfliegen v leave (plane)
der Abflug departure (plane)
abgeben v place (a bet)
abheben v withdraw (money)
die Abhebung withdrawal (bank)
abholen v pick up (something)
ablehnen v decline (credit card)
abmelden v log off (computer)
der Abschleppwagen tow truck
abschließen v lock (door)
der Adapter adapter
die Adresse n address
das Aftershave aftershave
die Agentur agency
AIDS AIDS
die Akupunktur n acupuncture
akzeptieren v accept
allein alone; **~stehend** single (person)
allergisch allergic;
die allergische

Reaktion allergic reaction
alt adj old
das Alter n age
die Alternativroute alternate route
die Aluminiumfolie aluminum [kitchen BE] foil
amerikanisch American
die Ampel traffic light
anämisch anemic
die Anästhesie anesthesia
der Anfänger beginner/ novice
angreifen v attack
anhalten v stop
der Anhänger trailer
ankommen arrive
die Ankunft arrival
anmelden v log on (computer)
der Anruf n call
anrufen v call
anschalten v turn on (device)
ansteckend contagious
das Antibiotikum n antibiotic
das Antiquitätengeschäft antiques store
antiseptisch antiseptic
der Anwalt lawyer
die Anzahlung n deposit (car rental)
der Anzug n suit
das Apartment apartment

die Apotheke pharmacy
[chemist BE]
arbeiten v work
arbeitslos adj unemployed
der Arm n arm (body part)
die Aromatherapie aromatherapy
die Arterie artery
die Arthritis arthritis
der Arzt doctor
asiatisch Asian
das Aspirin aspirin
asthmatisch asthmatic
atmen breathe (place)
attraktiv attractive
auf Wiedersehen goodbye
aufladen v recharge
das Auge eye
ausbessern v mend (clothing)
der Ausfluss discharge (bodily
fluid)
ausfüllen v fill out (form)
der Ausgang n exit
ausgeschlafen well-rested
die Auskunft information
(phone)
die Ausrüstung equipment
ausschalten turn off (device)
der Ausschlag rash
der Aussichtsplatz viewpoint
[BE]
aussprechen pronounce
aussteigen get off (a train/
bus/subway)
Australien Australia

der Australier Australian
das Auto car; ~ **mit
Automatikschaltung**
automatic car; ~ **mit
Gangschaltung** manual car
die Autobahn highway
[motorway BE]
automatisch automatic
der Autositz car seat
die Autovermietung car
rental [hire BE]

B

das Baby baby
die Babyflasche baby bottle
die Babynahrung formula
(baby)
das Baby-Pflegetuch baby
wipe
der Babysitter babysitter
backen bake
die Bäckerei bakery
das Bad bathroom
der Badeanzug swimsuit
die Badelatschen flip-flops
der Bahnhof train [railway BE]
station
der Bahnsteig track [platform
BE]
das Ballett ballet
die Bank bank (money)
der Bankautomat ATM
die Bankkarte ATM card
die Bar bar (place)
das Bargeld n cash

der Baseball baseball (game)

der Basketball basketball (game)

die Batterie battery

die Bauchschmerzen stomachache

der Bauernhof n farm

der Baum tree

die Baumwolle cotton

die Beaufsichtigung supervision

die Bedienung service (in a restaurant)

beenden v exit (computer)

beginnen begin

behindert handicapped; **~engerecht** handicapped [disabled BE]-accessible

beige adj beige

die Beilage side order

das Bein leg

beinhalten include (tax)

die Bekleidung clothing

das Bekleidungsgeschäft clothing store

belasten v charge (credit card)

belästigen bother

die Belichtung exposure (film)

benachrichtigen notify

benutzen v use

der Benutzername username

das Benzin gas [petrol BE]

beobachten v watch

der Berater consultant

berauben rob

beraubt robbed

bereit ready

der Berg hill; ~ mountain

beschädigen v damage

beschädigt damaged

die Beschwerde complaint

die Beschwerden condition (medical)

der Besen broom

die Besichtigungstour sightseeing tour

besser better

bestätigen confirm

beste adj best

bestellen v order (restaurant)

besuchen v visit

die Besuchszeiten visiting hours

das Bett n bed

die Bettwäsche sheets

bewusstlos unconscious (condition)

bezahlen pay

die Beziehung relationship

der BH bra

der Bikini bikini

billig cheap

billiger cheaper

bitte please

die Blase bladder

blau adj blue

bleifrei unleaded (gas)

der Blinddarm appendix

(body part)
der Blindenhund guide dog
das Blitzlicht flashlight
die Blume n flower
die Bluse blouse
das Blut blood
der Blutdruck blood pressure
bluten bleed
der Blutstau congestion
das Boot boat
die Bordkarte boarding pass
der botanische
  Garten botanical garden
der Boxkampf boxing match
die Bratpfanne frying pan
brauchen v need
braun adj brown
brechen v break
die Bremse brakes (car)
brennen v burn
der Brief letter
der Briefkasten mailbox
  [postbox BE]
die Briefmarke n stamp
  (postage)
die Brille glasses (optical)
bringen bring
britisch British
die Brosche brooch
die Brücke bridge
der Bruder brother
die Brust breast; ~ chest
  ~schmerzen chest pain
das Buch n book
die Bücherei library

der Buchladen bookstore
buchstabieren v spell
das Bügeleisen n iron
  (clothes)
bügeln v iron
das Büro office
die Bürozeiten office hours
der Bus bus; ~**bahnhof** bus
  station; ~**fahrschein** bus
  ticket
die Bushaltestelle bus stop;
die Business-Class business
  class
die Bustour bus tour

C

das Café cafe (place)
campen v camp
der Campingkocher camping
  stove
der Campingplatz campsite
die Campingtoilette chemical
  toilet
der Canyon canyon
das Casino casino
die CD CD
Celsius Celsius
das Check-in check-in
das Check-out check-out
chinesisch Chinese
der Club n club
der Computer computer
die Creme n cream (ointment)

D

danken thank
der Darm intestine
das (neuter) the
das Datum *n* date (calendar)
die Decke blanket
das Denkmal memorial (place)
das Deodorant deodorant
der the
das Deutsch German; **~land** Germany
der Diabetiker *n* diabetic
der Diamant diamond
die the
der Dieb thief; **~stahl** theft
diese this
der Diesel diesel
dieser this
dieses (neuter) this
digital digital
der Digitaldruck digital print
das Digitalfoto digital photo
die Digitalkamera digital camera
das Display *n* display
Dollar dollar (U.S.)
der Dolmetscher interpreter
das Doppelbett double bed
das Dorf village
dort there
der Dosenöffner can opener
draußen outside
dringend urgent

drucken *v* print
drücken *v* push
dunkel *adj* dark
der Durchfall diarrhea
durchreisen pass through
durstig thirsty
die Dusche *n* shower
das Dutzend dozen
die DVD DVD

E

echt real
die EC-Karte debit card
die Ecke *n* corner; **an der Ecke** on the corner
die Economy-Class economy class
die Ehefrau wife
der Ehemann husband
die Eile *n* rush
die Einbahnstraße one-way street
einbrechen *v* break in (burglary)
einchecken *v* check in
einführen *v* insert
der Eingang entrance
eingravieren engrave
der Einheimische *n* local (person)
einkaufen *v* shop
das Einkaufen shopping
der Einkaufskorb basket (grocery store)
der Einkaufswagen cart

[trolley BE] (grocery store)

das Einkaufszentrum
shopping mall [centre BE];
~ shopping area (town)

einlösen v cash (check)

einmal once

einpacken v wrap (parcel)

eins one

das Einschreiben registered
mail

einsteigen v board (bus)

eintreten v enter

der Eintritt admission (fee)

der Einwegartikel n
disposable

der Einweg-Rasierer
disposable razor

einzahlen v deposit (money)

die Einzahlung n deposit
(bank)

der Einzelabzug single print

das Einzelbett single bed

das Einzelzimmer single
room

das Eis n ice; **~hockey** ice
hockey

der Ellenbogen elbow

die E-Mail n e-mail;
~-Adresse e-mail address;
~ **senden** v e-mail

empfehlen recommend

die Empfehlung
recommendation

eng tight (fit)

englisch English

der Enkel grandchild

entleeren v empty

entschuldigen v excuse

entwerten v stamp (ticket)

entwickeln v develop (film)

epileptisch adj epileptic

erbrechen v vomit

erfahren adj experienced

erhalten receive

die Erkältung n cold
(sickness)

erklären explain

erlauben allow

ernst serious

erreichen v reach

erschöpft exhausted

erstaunlich amazing

erste Klasse first class

erste adj first

erwärmen v warm
(something)

essen eat

das Essen food

das Esszimmer dining room

die Etage floor [storey BE]

das E-Ticket e-ticket

etwas something;
~ **mehr...** some more...

der EU-Bürger EU resident

der Euro euro

die Exkursion excursion

der Experte n expert

der Express n express;
~bus express bus

extra extra; ~ **groß** extra

large

F

die **Fähre** ferry
fahren v drive
die **Fahrkarte** ticket
der **Fahrkartenschalter** ticket office
das **Fahrrad** n bicycle
der **Fahrradweg** bike route
der **Fahrstuhl** elevator [lift BE]
die **Fahrzeugregistrierung** vehicle registration
die **Familie** family
die **Farbe** n color
das **Fax** n fax
faxen v fax
die **Faxnummer** fax number
der **Fehler** n mistake
fehlen be missing
der **Urlaub** vacation [holiday BE]
das **Feinkostgeschäft** delicatessen
das **Fenster** window
der **Fernseher** television
das **Festpreismenü** fixed-price menu
die **Festung** fort
fettfrei fat free
das **Feuer** n fire
die **Feuertür** fire door
die **Feuerwehr** fire department
das **Feuerzeug** lighter

das **Fieber** fever
filetiert fileted (food)
der **Film** film (camera);
~ movie (cinema)
der **Finger** n finger
der **Fingernagel** fingernail
der **Fitnessraum** gym (workout)
die **Flasche** n bottle
der **Flaschenöffner** bottle opener
der **Fleischer** butcher
der **Florist** florist
der **Flug** flight
die **Fluggesellschaft** airline
der **Flughafen** airport
das **Flugzeug** airplane
der **Fluss** river
der **Fön** hair dryer
das **Förderband** conveyor belt
das **Formular** n form
fortgeschritten intermediate
das **Foto** photo
die **Fotografie** photography
fotografieren take a photo
die **Fotokopie** photocopy
die **Frage** n question
der **Franzbranntwein** rubbing alcohol [surgical spirit BE]
die **Frau** woman
freiberufliche Arbeit freelance work
frei adj free
das **Fremdenverkehrsbüro**

tourist information office
die Freude pleasure
der Freund boyfriend; friend
die Freundin girlfriend; friend
frisch fresh
die Frischhaltefolie plastic
wrap
der Friseur barber, hairstylist
der Friseursalon hair salon
die Frisur hairstyle
früh early
das Frühstück breakfast
der Führer guide
die Führerscheinnummer
driver's license number
das Fundbüro lost-and-found
für for
der Fuß foot; ~**ball** soccer
das Fußballspiel soccer
match [football game BE]
der Fußgänger *n* pedestrian
das Fußgelenk *n* ankle
füttern *v* feed

G

die Gabel fork
der Gang aisle
die Garage garage
das Gate gate (airport)
das Gebäude building
geben *v* give
die Gebühr fee
der Geburtstag birthday
gefährlich dangerous
der Gefrierschrank freezer

das Gegenteil *n* opposite
gehen *v* go (somewhere)
gekocht stewed
das Gel gel (hair)
gelb *adj* yellow
das Gelbgold yellow gold
das Geld money
die Geldbörse wallet
der Geldschein *n* bill [note
BE] (money)
das Gelenk joint (body part)
das Generikum generic drug
[unbranded medication BE]
genießen *v* enjoy
das Gepäck baggage
[luggage BE]
die Gepäckausgabe baggage
claim
der Gepäckschein baggage
[luggage BE] ticket
das Gepäckschließfach
baggage [luggage BE] locker
der Gepäckwagen baggage
[luggage BE] cart
geradeaus straight
gern geschehen you're
welcome
das Geschäft business;
~ store ~**sverzeichnis** store
directory;
~**szentrum** business center
das Geschenk gift
der Geschenkwarenladen
gift shop
das Geschirr dishes (kitchen)

der Geschirrspüler
dishwasher
das Geschirrspülmittel
dishwashing liquid
geschlossen closed
die Geschwindigkeitsüber-
schreitung speeding
das Gesicht *n* face
gestern yesterday
gestohlen stolen
die Gesundheit health
das Getränk *n* drink
die Getränkekarte drink
menu
getrennt lebend separated
(person)
das Gewitter thunderstorm
gewürfelt diced (food)
das Gift *n* poison
der Gipfel peak (of a
mountain)
das Girokonto checking
[current BE] account
das Glas glass
gleich same
glücklich happy
die Glühbirne lightbulb
golden golden
der Golfplatz golf course
das Golfturnier golf
tournament
das Grad degree
(temperature)
das Gramm gram
grau *adj* gray

der Grill *n* barbecue
groß big; ~ large
großartig magnificent
das Großbritannien United
Kingdom (U.K.)
die Größe *n* size
die Großeltern grandparents
größer bigger; ~ larger
grün *adj* green
die Gruppe *n* group
gültig valid
der Gürtel belt
gut *adj* good; *adv* well;
~**en Abend** good evening;
~**en Morgen** good morning;
~**en Tag** good day
der Gynäkologe gynecologist

H

das Haar hair
die Haarbürste hairbrush
der Harfestiger mousse (hair)
der Haarschnitt haircut
das Haarspray hairspray
haben *v* have
halal halal
halb half; ~**gar** underdone;
die ~**e Stunde** half hour;
das ~**e Kilo** half-kilo
die Halbschuhe loafers
halbtags part-time
das Hallenbad indoor pool
Hallo hello
der Hals throat
die Halsschmerzen sore

throat

die Haltestelle *n* stop

der Hammer *n* hammer

die Hand *n* hand

das Handgelenk wrist

das Handgepäck hand luggage

die Handtasche purse [handbag BE]

das Handtuch towel

Handwäsche hand wash

das Handy cell [mobile BE] phone

hässlich ugly

die Hauptattraktion main attraction

das Hauptgericht main course

das Haus *n* house

das Haushaltsgerät utensil

die Haushaltswaren household goods

die Haut *n* skin

heiraten *v* marry

heiß hot (temperature); **~e Quelle** hot spring; **~es Wasser** hot water

heizen *v* heat

die Heizung heating

der Hektar hectare

helfen *v* help

der Helm helmet

das Hemd shirt

der Herd stove

das Herz heart

die Herzkrankheit heart condition

der Heuschnupfen hay fever

heute today; **~ Abend** tonight

hier here

die Hilfe *n* help

die Hin- und Rückfahrt round-trip

Hinfahrt- one-way (ticket)

hinter behind (direction)

hoch high

das Hockey hockey

die Höhle *n* cave

hörgeschädigt hearing impaired

die Hose pants [trousers BE]

das Hotel hotel

hungrig hungry

husten *v* cough

der Husten *n* cough

der Hut hat

I

das Ibuprofen ibuprofen

die Identifikation identification

die Impfung vaccination

in in

infiziert infected

die Information information; **~** information desk

inländisch domestic

der Inlandsflug domestic flight

das Insekt bug
der Insektenschutz insect repellent
der Insektenstich insect bite
die Instant Message instant message
das Insulin insulin
interessant interesting
international international;
 der ~e Studentenausweis international student card;
 der ~e Flug international flight
das Internet internet;
 ~café internet cafe
der Internet-service internet service
irisch adj Irish
Irland Ireland
italienisch adj Italian

J

ja yes
die Jacke jacket
das Jahr year
japanisch Japanese
der Jazz jazz; **~club** jazz club
die Jeans jeans
der Jeansstoff denim
der Jet-ski jet ski
jetzt now
die Jugendherberge hostel;
 ~ youth hostel
jung adj young
der Junge boy

der Juwelier jeweler

K

das Kabarett cabaret
das Kaffeehaus coffee house
die Kalorie calorie
kalt adj cold (temperature);
 ~ cool (temperature)
die Kamera camera
die Kameratasche camera case
der Kamm n comb
das Kanada Canada
kanadisch adj Canadian
die Karaffe carafe
die Karte n card; **~** map
der Kassierer cashier
der Kater hangover (alcohol)
die Kathedrale cathedral
kaufen v buy
das Kaufhaus department store
der Kaugummi chewing gum
der Kellner waiter
die Kellnerin waitress
die Kette necklace
der Kiefer jaw
das Kilo kilo;
 ~gramm kilogram
der Kilometer kilometer
das Kind child
der Kinderarzt pediatrician
das Kinderbecken kiddie pool
das Kinderbett cot

die **Kinderkarte** children's menu

die **Kinderportion** children's portion

der **Kindersitz** highchair

der **Kinderstuhl** child's seat;

der **Kinderwagen** stroller

das **Kino** movie theater

die **Kirche** church

das **Kissen** pillow

die **Klarsichtfolie** plastic wrap [cling film BE]

die **Klasse** class

die **klassische Musik** classical music

das **Kleid** *n* dress (clothing)

die **Kleiderordnung** dress code

klein small

der **Kleintransporter** van

die **Klimaanlage** air conditioning

die **Klippe** cliff

das **Kloster** monastery

das **Knie** *n* knee

der **Knochen** *n* bone

kochen *v* boil; ~ cook

das **Kölnischwasser** cologne

der **Koffer** suitcase

der **Kollege** colleague

kommen *v* come

die **Konditorei** pastry shop

das **Kondom** condom

die **Konferenz** conference

das **Konferenzzimmer** meeting room

der **Kongressaal** convention hall

die **Konserve** canned good

das **Konsulat** consulate

kontaktieren *v* contact

die **Kontaktlinse** contact lens

die **Kontaktlinsenlösung** contact lens solution

das **Konto** *n* account

das **Konzert** concert

die **Konzerthalle** concert hall

der **Kopf** *n* head (body part)

die **Kopfhörer** headphones

die **Kopfschmerzen** headache

der **Korkenzieher** corkscrew

koscher kosher

kosmetisch *adj* cosmetic; ~e **Gesichtsbehandlung** facial (treatment)

kosten *v* cost; ~ taste

krank ill; ~ sick

das **Krankenhaus** hospital

die **Krankenschwester** *n* nurse

der **Krankenwagen** ambulance

die **Krawatte** tie (clothing)

die **Kreditkarte** credit card

die **Kreuzung** intersection

das **Kriegsdenkmal** war memorial

das **Kristall** crystal (glass)

die **Küche** kitchen

die **Küchenmaschine** food processor
der **Kühlschrank** refrigerator
die **Kunst** art
das **Kupfer** copper
kurz short; **~e Hose** shorts
kurzärmelig short-sleeved
kurzsichtig near- [short- BE] sighted
küssen v kiss

L

laktoseintolerant lactose intolerant
die **Lampe** n light (overhead)
die **Landesvorwahl** country code
landwirtschaftliches Erzeugnis produce
lang adj long; **~ärmlig** long-sleeved;
langsam slow; **~er** slower
langweilig boring
der **Laufstall** playpen
lauter louder
leben v live
das **Lebensmittelgeschäft** grocery store
die **Leber** liver (body part)
lecker delicious
das **Leder** leather
leicht easy
das **Leinen** linen
leise quiet

die **Lektion** lesson
letzte adj last
die **Liebe** n love
lieben v love (someone)
der **Liegestuhl** deck chair (ferry)
der **Liftpass** lift pass
die **Linie** line (train)
links left (direction)
die **Linse** lens
die **Lippe** lip
der **Liter** liter
Livemusik live music
locker loose (fit)
der **Löffel** n spoon
löschen v clear (on an ATM); **~** v delete (computer)
die **Lotion** lotion
die **Luftpost** n airmail
die **Luftpumpe** air pump
lufttrocknen v air dry
die **Lunge** lung

M

das **Mädchen** girl
das **Magazin** magazine
der **Magen** stomach
die **Magenverstimmung** upset stomach
die **Mahlzeit** meal
der **Manager** manager
die **Maniküre** n manicure
der **Mann** man (male)
der **Mantel** n coat

der **Markt** market
maschinentrocknen tumble dry
die **Massage** *n* massage
mechanisch *adj* mechanic
das **Medikament** medicine
die **Medikamente** medication
medium *adj* medium (meat)
das **Meer** sea
mehr more
die **Mehrwertsteuer** sales tax [VAT BE]
die **Menstruationskrämpfe** menstrual cramps
die **Messe** mass (church service)
messen *v* measure (someone)
das **Messer** knife
der **Messbecher** measuring cup
der **Messlöffel** measuring spoon
das **Mietauto** rental [hire BE] car
mieten *v* rent [hire BE]
die **Mikrowelle** *n* microwave
mild mild
die **Mini-Bar** mini-bar
die **Minute** minute
mit with; **~ Bedienung** full-service
die **Mitgliedskarte** membership card
mitkommen *v* join
mitnehmen give somebody a

lift (ride)
Mittag noon [midday BE]
das **Mittagessen** *n* lunch
Mitternacht midnight
der **Mixer** blender
die **Mobilität** mobility
mögen *v* like
der **Monat** month
die **Monatsbinde** sanitary napkin [pad BE]
der **Mopp** *n* mop
das **Moped** moped
morgen tomorrow
der **Morgen** morning
die **Moschee** mosque
der **Moslem** Muslim
das **Motorboot** motor boat
das **Motorrad** motorcycle
das **Mountainbike** mountain bike
müde tired
der **Mund** mouth
die **Münze** coin
das **Münztelefon** pay phone
das **Museum** museum
die **Musik** music
das **Musikgeschäft** music store
der **Muskel** muscle
die **Mutter** mother

N

nach after
der **Nachmittag** afternoon
nachprüfen *v* check (on

something)

die Nachricht message

nachschneiden trim (haircut)

nächste *adj* next

die Nacht night

der Nachtclub nightclub

der Nacken neck

die Nagelfeile nail file

das Nagelstudio nail salon

nahe *prep* near

die Nähe vicinity;
  in der Nähe nearby

der Name *n* name

die Nase nose

die Nationalität nationality

das Naturreservat nature preserve

die Nebenstelle extension (phone)

die Nebenwirkung side effect

nehmen *v* take

nein no

Nichtraucher- non-smoking (area)

nichts nothing

niedrig low

die Niere kidney (body part)

der Norden *n* north

normal regular

der Notausgang emergency exit

der Notfall emergency

die Nummer *n* number

nur only; ~ just

O

obere *adj* upper

der Oberschenkel thigh

offen *adj* open

öffentlich *adj* public

öffnen *v* open

die Öffnungszeiten business hours

ohne without

das Ohr ear

die Ohrenschmerzen earache

der Ohrring earring

OK okay

das Öl *n* oil

die Oper opera

das Opernhaus opera house

der Optiker optician

orange *adj* orange (color)

das Orchester orchestra

die Ortsvorwahl area code

der Osten *n* east

P

packen *v* pack

die Packung carton;
  ~ packet

das Paket package

der Palast palace

paniert breaded

die Panne breakdown (car)

die Pantoffeln slippers

das Papier *n* paper

das Papierhandtuch paper towel

das Paracetamol
acetaminophen
[paracetamol BE]

das Parfüm *n* perfume

der Park *n* park

parken *v* park

das Parkhaus parking garage

der Parkplatz parking lot [car
park BE]

die Parkuhr parking meter

das Parlamentsgebäude
parliament building

das Parterre ground floor

der Passagier passenger

die Passform fit (clothing)

die Passkontrolle passport
control

das Passwort password

die Pediküre pedicure

das Penicillin penicillin

der Penis penis

die Pension bed and
breakfast

die Periode period
(menstrual)

die Perle pearl

der Pfad path

die Pferderennbahn
horsetrack

das Pflaster bandage

das Pfund *n* pound (weight)

das Pfund pound (British
sterling)

die Pille Pill (birth control)

die Piste *n* trail [piste BE]

der Pistenplan trail [piste
BE] map

die Pizzeria pizzeria

der Plan *n* schedule
[timetable BE]; ~ map

planen *v* plan

das Platin platinum

der Platte flat tire

der Platz field (sports); ~ seat;
~ am Gang aisle seat

die Plombe filling (tooth)

der Po buttocks

die Polizei police

der Polizeibericht police
report

das Polizeirevier police
station

der Pool *n* pool

die Popmusik pop music

die Portion *n* portion

die Post mail [post BE]; ~ post
office

die Postkarte postcard

der Preis price;
~ pro Gedeck cover charge

preisgünstig inexpensive

pro per; ~ **Nacht** per night;
~ **Stunde** per hour; ~
Tag per day; ~ **Woche** per
week

das Problem problem

Prost! Cheers!

die Prothese denture

die Puppe doll

der Pyjama pajamas

Q

die Qualität *n* quality
die Quittung receipt

R

das R-Gespräch collect call [reverse charge call BE]
ein R-Gespräch führen *v* call collect [to reverse the charges BE]
der Rabatt discount
das Radfahren cycling
der Rap rap (music)
die Rasiercreme shaving cream
die Rasierklinge razor blade
der Rastplatz picnic area
das Rathaus town hall
der Rathausplatz town square
rauchen *v* smoke
Raucher- smoking (area)
die Rechnung bill [invoice BE] (of sale)
rechts right (direction)
das Recycling recycling
das Reformhaus health food store
der Regen *n* rain
die Regenjacke raincoat
der Regenschirm umbrella
der Regenwald rainforest
die Region region
regnerisch rainy

der Reifen tire [tyre BE]
reinigen *v* clean;
chemisch ~ dry clean
die Reinigung dry cleaner's
die Reinigungsmittel cleaning supplies
die Reise trip; ~ journey
das Reisebüro travel agency
der Reiseführer guide book
die Reisekrankheit motion sickness
der Reisepass passport
der Reisescheck traveler's check [cheque BE]
die Rennbahn racetrack
der Rentner senior citizen
reparieren *v* fix; ~ repair
reservieren *v* reserve
die Reservierung reservation
der Reservierungsschalter reservation desk
das Restaurant restaurant
der Rettungsschwimmer lifeguard
das Rezept prescription
die Rezeption reception
die Richtung direction
der Ring *n* ring
die Rippe rib (body part)
der Rock skirt
der Rollstuhl wheelchair
die Rollstuhlrampe wheelchair ramp

die **Rolltreppe** escalator
romantisch romantic
rosa adj pink
rot adj red
die **Route** route
der **Rücken** n back (body part)
die **Rückenschmerzen** backache
der **Rucksack** backpack
das **Ruderboot** rowboat
das **Rugby** rugby
die **Ruine** ruin

S

der **Safe** n safe (for valuables)
die **Sandalen** sandals
sauber adj clean
die **Sauerstoffbehandlung** oxygen treatment
die **Saugglocke** plunger
die **Sauna** sauna
der **Scanner** scanner
die **Schachtel** n pack; ~ **Zigaretten** pack of cigarettes
der **Schal** scarf
scharf hot (spicy); ~ sharp
das **Schaufenster** window case
der **Scheck** n check [cheque BE] (payment)
die **Schere** scissors
schicken send; **per Post ~** mail
das **Schlachtfeld** battleground
schlafen v sleep
die **Schläfrigkeit** drowsiness
der **Schlafsack** sleeping bag
die **Schlafstörung** insomnia
der **Schlafwagen** sleeper [sleeping BE] car
der **Schläger** racket (sports)
schlecht nauseous; ~ bad
der **Schlepplift** drag lift
schließen v close (a shop)
das **Schließfach** locker
das **Schloss** castle; ~ lock
die **Schlucht** ravine
der **Schlüssel** key; **~ring** key ring
die **Schlüsselkarte** key card
der **Schmerz** pain; **Schmerzen haben** be in pain
der **Schmuck** jewelry
schmutzig dirty
der **Schneeschuh** snowshoe
schneiden v cut
schnell fast
der **Schnellzug** express train
der **Schnitt** n cut (injury)
der **Schnuller** pacifier [soother BE]
schön nice; ~ beautiful
schrecklich terrible
schreiben write
der **Schrein** shrine
der **Schuh** shoe
das **Schuhgeschäft** shoe store

die Schule school
die Schulter shoulder
die Schüssel bowl
schwanger pregnant
schwarz *adj* black
die Schwellung swelling
die Schwester sister
schwierig difficult
das Schwimmbad swimming pool
schwimmen *v* swim
die Schwimmweste life jacket
schwindelig dizzy
schwul *adj* gay
die Schwulenbar gay bar
der Schwulenclub gay club
der See lake
sehbehindert visually impaired
sehen *v* look; ~ see
die Sehenswürdigkeit attraction
die Seide silk
die Seife *n* soap
die Seilbahn cable car
sein *v* be
die Selbstbedienung self-service
selten rare
seltsam strange
das Seminar seminar
senden *v* send
die Serviette napkin
der Sessellift chair lift

sexuell übertragbare Krankheit sexually transmitted disease (STD)
das Shampoo *n* shampoo
sich scheiden lassen *v* divorce
sicher *adj* safe (protected)
die Sicherheit security
das Sieb colander
das Sightseeing sightseeing
das Silber *n* silver
sitzen *v* sit
der Ski *n* ski
Ski fahren *v* ski
der Skilift ski lift
der Slip briefs (clothing)
die SMS SMS;
eine SMS schicken *v* text (message)
das Snowboard *n* snowboard
die Socke sock
die Sonne *n* sun
der Sonnenbrand sunburn
die Sonnenbrille sunglasses
die Sonnencreme sunscreen
der Sonnenstich sunstroke
sonnig sunny
das Souvenir souvenir;
~geschäft souvenir store
das Sparkonto savings (account)
spät late (time)
der Spatel spatula
später later
spazieren gehen *v* walk

der **Spaziergang** *n* walk

die **Speicherkarte** memory card

speichern *v* save (computer)

die **Speisekarte** menu

der **Spezialist** specialist (doctor)

das **Spiel** game; ~ match

spielen *v* play

die **Spielhalle** arcade

der **Spielplatz** playground

das **Spielzeug** toy

der **Spielzeugladen** toy store

das **Spirituosengeschäft** liquor store [off-licence BE]

die **Spitze** lace (fabric)

der **Sport** sports

die **Sportmassage** sports massage

das **Sportgeschäft** sporting goods store

sprechen *v* speak

der **Springbrunnen** fountain

die **Spülung** conditioner (hair)

die **Stäbchen** chopsticks

das **Stadion** stadium

die **Stadt** city; ~ town

der **Stadtplan** town map

die **Stadtrundfahrt** sightseeing tour

das **Stadtzentrum** downtown area

die **Stange** carton (of cigarettes)

die **Statue** statue

der **Staubsauger** vacuum cleaner

das **Steakhouse** steakhouse

die **Steckdose** electric outlet

stehlen *v* steal

steil steep

das **Sterlingsilber** sterling silver

der **Stich** *n* sting

die **Stiefel** boots

der **Stift** pen

stillen breastfeed

die **Stöcke** poles (skiing)

stornieren *v* cancel

die **Strafe** *n* fine (fee for breaking law)

die **Strähnchen** highlights (hair)

der **Strand** beach

die **Straßenkarte** road map

der **Strom** electricity

die **Strumpfhose** pantyhose [tights BE]

das **Stück** *n* piece; ~ play (theater); ~ slice

der **Student** student

studieren *v* study

der **Stuhl** chair

der **Stuhlgang** stool (bowel movement)

die **Stunde** hour

der **Süden** *n* south

das **Super** super (fuel)

der Supermarkt supermarket
das Surfboard surfboard
das Surfbrett windsurfer (board)
süß cute; ~ sweet (taste)
die Süßigkeit candy [sweet BE]
das Sweatshirt sweatshirt
die Synagoge synagogue
synchronisiert dubbed

T

der Tabakhändler tobacconist
die Tablette tablet (medicine)
der Tag day
Tages- one-day (ticket)
das Tal valley
der Tampon tampon
tanken v fill (car)
die Tankstelle gas [petrol BE] station
der Tanzclub dance club
tanzen v dance
die Tasche bag; ~ pocket
die Tasse n cup
taub adj deaf
die Tauchausrüstung diving equipment
tauchen v dive
das Taxi taxi
das Team team
der Teelöffel teaspoon
der Teich pond
das Teil part (for car)

das Telefon n phone
das schnurlose Telefon wireless phone
der Telefonanruf phone call
die Telefonkarte phone card
die Telefonnummer phone number
der Teller plate
der Tempel temple (religious)
das Tennis tennis
der Termin appointment
der Terminal terminal (airport)
teuer expensive
der Text n text
das Theater theater
tief deep
die Tiefkühlkost frozen food
das Tier animal
der Tisch table
die Toilette restroom [toilet BE]
das Toilettenpapier toilet paper
der Topf n pot
die Töpferwaren pottery (pots)
die Tour n tour
der Tourist tourist
traditionell traditional
traurig sad
treffen meet
das Treffen meeting
trennen disconnect (computer)

die Treppe stairs
trinken v drink
das Trinkwasser drinking water
der Tropfen n drop (medicine)
das T-Shirt T-shirt
die Tür door
der Turm tower
die Turnschuhe sneaker

U

die U-Bahn subway [underground BE]
die U-Bahn-Haltestelle subway [underground BE] station
über prep over;
~ **Nacht** overnight;
~**fallen** v mug
die Übergröße plus size
überhitzen overheat (car)
übersetzen translate
überweisen v transfer (money)
um (die Ecke) around (the corner)
umändern alter
umarmen v hug
die Umkleidekabine fitting room
der Umschlag envelope
umsteigen v change (buses);
~ v transfer (change trains/ flights)
umtauschen v exchange

(money)
umwerfend stunning
unbeaufsichtigt unattended
der Unfall accident
die Universität university
die Unterhaltung entertainment (amusement)
die Unterhose underwear [underpants BE]
die Unterkunft accommodation
die Unterlegplane groundcloth
unterschreiben v sign
der Untertitel n subtitle
die Unterwäsche underwear
der Urin urine
der Urlaub vacation [BE holiday]

V

die Vagina vagina
vaginal vaginal; **die ~e Entzündung** vaginal infection
der Vater father
der V-Ausschnitt V-neck
der Veganer n vegan
der Vegetarier n vegetarian
der Ventilator fan (appliance)
verbieten v prohibit
verbinden v connect (internet)
die Verbindung connection
die Vereinigten Staaten United States (U

verfügbar available
vergewaltigen *v* rape
die Vergewaltigung *n* rape
der
  Vergnügungspark amusement park
verheiratet married
verkaufen *v* sell
verlangen *v* charge (cost)
verlieren *v* lose (something)
verlobt engaged
verloren lost
verschlucken *v* swallow
verschneit snowy
verschreiben *v* prescribe (medication)
versenden *v* ship
die Versicherung insurance
**die Versicherungs-
  gesellschaft** insurance company
die Versicherungskarte insurance card
die Verstauchung *n* sprain
verstehen understand
die Verstopfung constipation
verwitwet widowed
verzögern *v* delay
viel much; ~ a lot;
  ~en Dank thank you;
  wie ~ how much
violett *adj* purple
die Visitenkarte business card
das Visum visa

das Vitamin vitamin
die Vitrine display case
der Vogel bird
die Volksmusik folk music
das Volleyballspiel volleyball game
Vollzeit- full-time
vor before; **Viertel ~ vier** a quarter to four
die Vorfahrt right of way
die Vorhersage *n* forecast
die Vorspeise appetizer [starter BE]
vorstellen *v* introduce (person)
vorübergehend temporary

W

wählen *v* dial
während during
die Währung currency
der Währungsumtausch currency exchange
der Wald forest
die Wanderroute walking route
die Wanderschuhe hiking boots
die Wanduhr wall clock
wann when (time)
die Ware *n* good; ~ product
die Waren goods
warm *adj* warm (temperature)
warten wait
der Warteraum waiting room

die **Wartezeit** n waiting
period
was what
das **Waschbecken** n sink
die **Wäscherei** laundry
(facility)
der **Wäscheservice** laundry
service
die **Waschmaschine** washing
machine
waschmaschinenfest
machine washable
das **Waschmittel** detergent
der **Waschsalon** laundromat
[launderette BE]
der **Wasserfall** waterfall
die **Wasserski** water skis
das **Wechselgeld** n change
(money)
der **Wechselkurs** exchange
rate
wechseln v change
die **Wechselstube** currency
exchange office
wecken v wake
der **Weckruf** wake-up call
weich soft
das **Weingut** vineyard
die **Weinkarte** wine list
weiß adj white
das **Weißgold** white gold
weit adv far (distance);
~ adj loose (fit)
weitsichtig far [long BE]-
sighted

das **Wellness-Center** spa
wenig adj little (not much)
weniger less
wer who
der **Wert** value
wertvoll valuable
der **Westen** n west
das **Wetter** weather
wickeln v change (baby)
wie how; ~ **viel** how much
wiederholen repeat
willkommen adj welcome
die **Windel** diaper [nappy BE]
die **Wirbelsäule** spine (body
part)
wireless wireless
wo where
die **Woche** week
das **Wochenende** weekend
wöchentlich weekly
der **Wohnwagen** mobile
home
die **Wolle** wool
wunder schön beautiful
die **Wüste** n desert

Z

der **Zahn** tooth
der **Zahnarzt** dentist
die **Zahnpaste** toothpaste
der **Zeh** n toe
der **Zehennagel** toenail
das **Zeichen** symbol
(keyboard)
zeigen v show (somebody

something)
die Zeit time
der Zeitraum period (of time)
die Zeitung newspaper
der Zeitungskiosk newsstand
das Zelt tent
der Zelthering tent peg
die Zeltstange tent pole
der Zentimeter centimeter
zerbrochen broken
  (smashed)
das Zertifikat certificate
ziehen v extract (tooth);
  ~ v pull (door sign)
die Zigarette cigarette
die Zigarre cigar
das Zimmer room
der Zimmerschlüssel room
  key
der Zimmerservice room
  service
das Zinn pewter
der Zoll customs; ~ duty (tax)
zollfrei duty-free
der Zoo zoo
zu adv too; ~ prep to
der Zug train
die Zunge tongue
zurückgeben v return
  (something)
der Zutritt n access